Everlasting Love

Living the Rock 'n Roll Dream with Buzz Cason

To Eric,
Great Meeting you
and seeing you studio
thanks for you

Buzz Cason

help!
Blessings
and Rock ON!

Buzz Cason 2015

Published by Premiere

Contents

FOREWORD BY BRENDA LEE

One of the most intriguing things about the beginnings of the rock-'n'-roll wild-fire was how quickly it spread. It seemed within a matter of weeks after the opening drumbeat of Bill Haley's "Rock Around the Clock" that teenage bands were everywhere. And it turned out that I joined forces with the first one ever formed in Music City.

Poking fun at their frenetic performance style, The Casuals, with lead singer Buzz Cason, began barnstorming the mid-South and became the talk of the town. The local notoriety of their hit disc, "My Love Song for You," led to The Casuals' first headlining tour in 1957. And that's how I came to meet them.

In November of that year, The Casuals were booked on a tour with musical comics Lonzo & Oscar, cowgirl singer Judy Lynn, and others. As a twelve-year-old with my first records on the market, I was on that tour too. I didn't have a band of my own, so my manager asked The Casuals if they'd like to back me up. They said, "Yes," and later signed on as my regular band in early 1958. That's how it started.

I remember that first tour with Buzz and The Casuals as being a total blast. We were a good little package, because we didn't just stand there and sing. With Buzz jumping all over the stage with a tambourine, it was energetic to say the least, and the audiences ate it up.

Left to Right: Chester Power, Brenda Lee (age eleven), Buzz and Richard Williams on stage in 1957.

And that was just the beginning. We hit the ground running and didn't look back. By 1960, I had my own repertoire of hits to perform. The Casuals had "My Love

Song for You." Then Buzz got a hit of his own. Under the name "Garry Miles," Buzz's version of "Look For A Star" sailed into the Top 20. And as if that weren't enough, Buzz and keyboardist Richard Williams teamed up with Hugh Jarrett of The Jordanaires to record as The Statues. So, rocking Buzz was a Casual and a Statue and was also Garry Miles. And there was to be no stopping him. Over the years, Buzz became a studio owner, hit songwriter, publisher, and ad jingle vocalist. But most importantly, Buzz has remained my dear friend. What happened to us in the beginning could never happen again. And I feel kind of sorry for the rock-'n'-rollers of today. Buzz, I'll bet they're not having nearly as much fun as we did! Thank you for a lifetime of friendship and memories. I join everyone in celebrating your living of the rock-'n'-roll dream.

Introduction

The spirit of rock 'n roll is the joy of the music: listening and performing it freely, sometimes living on the edge, and always dancing your heart out. It's that pent-up rebel attitude trying to break out of the restrictions and structure of everyday life. It is freedom itself!

It has been an absolute thrill to not only experience adventures of my early days in music, but to relive those rocking days and nights again. The friends, the fellow entertainers, and the places we played have etched a permanent smile in my heart and if I may, an everlasting love for music itself. The beautiful part is that many of these friendships have lasted over several decades, and as a bonus, many of our original artist friends still get together for oldie shows, writers' nights, reunion shows and even class reunions. What fun!

I'll be forever grateful for Keith, Mary, Brad, John, Richard, Belinda, Staci, and all the Hal Leonard team for for all the positive support and friendship during the process of bringing my the original version of my story to the public. Special thanks to Guy Gilchrist, of "Nancy" cartoon fame and an accompished songwriter, for introducing me to his agent, Bruce Butterfield, who was kind enough to take me on as a client. Gratitude to Bruce for making the connection with Fast Pencil and Steve Wilson, Michael Ashley, Mike Bertoldo and Tracy Wickham for their assistance and valuable input and bringing this book to life! And to Aaron Brown, who has been in the middle of so many of these adventures! Love you, man! Thanks for the encouragement. I am also appreciative of my assistants, Wanda Pojar, and Patricia Albrecht for their dedication and help in the organization and completion of this book. There are so many folks to thank. It would take several pages to list all those beloved friends who have meant so much to me and remain supportive and helpful in all I endeavor to do. To Vickie and all my family, for allowing me all those hours of hiding out to write, I'll be ever thankful. I love you all!

Things have changed since the less anxious and simpler days in which I started out. For those of you who lived through the rockin' '50s and '60s, perhaps these stories will trigger memorable incidents of your own from those days. And to the younger readers, I hope you will enjoy this close-up look at life in the early days of rock music. Although it was definitely a more innocent era of life then, to us the whole scene loomed larger than life.

"A ship in a harbor is safe," an ancient sage once said, "but that's not what ships are for," he added. If you have talent and dreams of success, you must leave your comfort zone, go out, and cultivate and exploit your gift. Comedian Jonathan Winters put it in a more contemporary way, "If your ship doesn't come in, swim out to it!" The young rockers I ran with fearlessly jumped out in the stream and loved every minute of it!

So, join me now for a ride down a two-lane highway in a shiny black Chevy station wagon, filled with six wide-eyed young passengers pulling a trailer filled with guitars, amplifiers, and drums as we set out to entertain folks all over the country.

Buzz Cason

Radio Dreamin' on Ardee Avenue

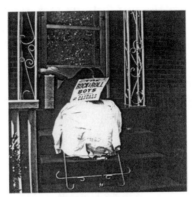

Rock 'n Roll boys,
home from a road trip

We were so young and free down on Ardee Avenue.
"Ardee Avenue" by Buzz Cason

The first time I can recall anyone suggesting that I participate in singing any other kind of music other than church hymns was when my neighborhood friend, Lewis Dale told me about this thing they called "hillbilly music" that was so popular on radio WSM's Grand Ole Opry. "We'll do our own radio show in my garage," declared the skinny kid who lived on the street behind our house. He lived about four houses down from me, one street over on Sunnymeade. After all, we lived in Inglewood, a musical neighborhood, with some known musicians and entertainers living on my street, Ardee Avenue. It was home to none other than Billy Byrd, who was Ernest Tubb's lead guitarist, and "Bunny" Biggs of the comedy blackface team Jamup and Honey, who like Byrd and Tubb, appeared on the Opry. Not only WSM Radio had live country on the air back then, but other Nashville stations had studios and broadcast fifteen- and thirty-minute shows. I recall hearing Big Jeff and the Radio Playboys on my mother's little red plastic radio she listened to in the kitchen. The legendary Roy Acuff and piano player Del Wood also lived near us, and to top that, Hank Williams's mother lived on Ardee just a few houses up from my best buddy, Aaron Brown. Hank was occasionally seen crawling out of his big Cadillac to visit his mom.

Roy Cason did not like hillbilly or as some folks north of Dixie referred to as "Countrywestern." That's right, one word, pronounced in a rather generic way with a Midwestern dialect. Roy was my father, a Renaissance man born in 1903, before airplanes flew and when automobiles and telephones were rare. By World War II, he was into the big bands. I never heard him mention being a fan of any particular singer, pop or otherwise. But he did love the orchestras. As the sun would set on a Sunday afternoon, he would lean back in his easy chair and listen to Guy Lombardo and smoke a cigarette. I'm convinced those whiny saxophones with all that vibrato did some kind of damage to the "musical memory" part of my brain, because I could never stand that sound for years after that. Since I was pretty much fascinated with anything that came over the airwaves at that time, I did listen with interest and managed to pick up on what was happening musically, despite the horn section.

My first encounter with live music came at the urging of Lewis Dale. Lewis was from Livingston, Tennessee, and a little more of a country boy than most of us. He really liked country music, and it was his bright idea that we start our own show in his garage. It sounded like a fun concept to me although I had no idea how we would do it.

"Ya know that song, 'I'm Throwing Rice at the Girl that I Love?' That's one we can do!" Lewis insisted. I didn't know that one or many country songs of the day, and unlike many singers and writers you hear about now who cut their teeth listening to the Opry, the Cason family didn't exactly huddle around the radio on Saturday nights glued to WSM.

"We'll call it the 'Hillbilly Opry,'" Lewis announced. He had in his possession a Stella guitar, which was one of the cheapest acoustic instruments a picker could buy then. It sounded cheap too. It probably would have helped if we had known how to tune it. But we had to start somewhere. I helped devise a washtub bass that sounded a lot worse than the real store-bought guitar. We then faced another glaring problem: none of us knew how to play an instrument. That hurt our plans for a full-blown neighborhood radio show tremendously, compounded by the fact that all of us kids got in a big fight over who would be the featured singer. Needless to say, our show never got off the ground, especially after we discovered that Mary Claire Minardi's rather risque burlesque revue was much more appealing to our potential audience. Mary Claire was a nice Catholic girl and the solo star of her own show, which featured a dance routine that included sidestepping by the onlookers, flipping her dress up, and giving the kids, especially us nine-year-old boys a thrill!

My mother, Rosa Jordan Cason, taught me to sing harmony notes without ever giving me one single lesson. We had attended Inglewood Baptist Church since moving to Ardee in the Edgefield development from our first home on Joseph Avenue in East Nashville, very near the Cumberland River and the budding downtown section of the city. When my mother wasn't singing in the choir, we would sit together and I would follow along as she harmonized in a sweet alto voice. Even in church today, I can almost hear that part being sung in my head, regardless of which part I might be singing. From the time I was sixteen until now I have been singing background parts on countless sessions, having been blessed with the ability to sing vocal parts from bass to a sometimes screaming falsetto. In my teens, as I read and heard about the early careers of the pop and rhythm-and-blues singers I admired so,

I discovered that singers like Clyde McPhatter, Ray Charles, and Elvis Presley had roots deep in church and gospel music. Many of the successful recording groups of the early rhythm-and-blues and rock era met each other in the church setting and went on to perform together for years to come. The piano lessons I received from Mrs. Nell Smith also included learning to play hymns along with classical selections and an occasional march piece we ten- and eleven-year-old students would struggle through. Just going over to Mrs. Smith's home on a nearby street provided unique challenge. The problem was next door to Mrs. Smith. His name was Billy Morgan. Billy was a bully. I was small and not a real good fighter, but after Billy discovered I would fight back and kick him in places he wasn't prepared for, we reached sort of a truce. It seemed he needed a friend. Most bullies don't make friends easily. I had inherited my mother's gift of gab and could usually talk or laugh my way out of most situations. Here is a tip in case you are ever on your back with a bully on top of you: arch your back as far up as you can and try to kick him or her in the back of the head. In addition, did you know that if you spit in a bully's face he usually releases his grip around your neck to wipe his eyes, thus providing you with a better opportunity to escape? This leads to what might be the best suggestion of all, that is to practice running fast. Unfortunately for me, Billy was pretty quick and could tackle fairly well, but I lived to tell about it. I don't know what ever happened to Billy, but the piano lessons my parents provided for me gave me a foundation in reading music and many lovely melodies were imprinted in the creative section of my brain. Also, the four-note suspended chords within the structure of hymns would later be integral parts in the composition of many of the songs I would later write.

What creative ability I'm blessed to have is a great deal due to my father's many talents. I've wished many times that I had inherited his gift of carpentry. He could build and fix up almost anything. He built sailboats, small fishing boats, and toy Jeeps for the war effort. He built fences and coops for our chickens. One of my favorite memories is that of fetching eggs for breakfast from our combination garage-henhouse. Reaching in the straw for those warm, soon-to-be-tasty eggs was really a fun chore. Roy Cason would build and carve furniture and other craft items for our family and friends. Many of the pieces of furniture he built fifty or so years ago are still in use today, sturdy, and looking like new. He built a mother-in-law house for my grandmother, Molly "Mama" Jordan, that also served as a Cub Scout Den for the boys of our neighborhood. One project he did for me was wiring up an antenna for a little red crystal radio I had received for Christmas when I was twelve years old. The thin wire ran outside my bedroom window, up under the gutter along the rear of our little brick house and soon brought a new world to my ears.

The voice that fascinated my teenage ears the most was that of Gene Nobles's. Along with Bill (Hoss) Allen, Herman Grizzard, and John (John R.) Richbourg, Gene was a deejay on the 50,000-watt WLAC Radio, the radio station originally owned by the Life and Casualty Insurance Company, thus the call letters

The Cason side of the family, Lebanon, Tennesse, about 1940. On far left, Buzz's mother Rosa Cason, Buzz, sister Sally Jo, and Father Roy (fifth from the right) along with numerous aunts, uncles, cousins, and in the front center, Grandmother Sara Reynolds

Gene had a unique, almost perverted-sounding, squelched announcing voice that drew the listener in. He came on around nine, six nights a week and like the other jocks he sold everything from baby chicks to 45- and 78-rpm records. Gene was the main pitchman for Randy's Record Shop of Gallatin, Tennessee. Randy Wood was the shop owner who also owned Dot Records, the label that would later release the first two records of my career. In the mid to late '50s, Dot was known for its hits by the Hilltoppers, Gale Storm, Billy Vaughn, Pat Boone, and one of the great rockabilly singles, "The Fool" by Sanford Clark. These records were mainly pop, but WLAC played blues and early R&B almost exclusively. Gene got away with some pretty strong language for those days. "That's hunchin' music," he'd say after playing a slow blues by such artists as Lowell Fulson and Bobby "Blue" Bland. He also loved to talk about gambling on the ponies down in Hot Springs, Arkansas. Listening to Gene was fun and sometimes shocking to a Southern Baptist boy but the music was really why I listened. Artists I heard for the first time included Jimmy Reed with "Baby What You Want Me to Do," Joe "The Boss of the Blues" Turner with "Shake, Rattle & Roll," LaVern Baker singing "Bop-Ting-a-Ling," Muddy Waters wailing "I'm a Man," Little Willie John's "Fever," and two Sun Records artists, Jerry Lee Lewis and Billy Lee Riley. Little did I know I would soon be working shows with this pair of hard rockin' artists.

Sun was owned by Sam Phillips. His brother Judd loved to come around to the stations with his famous "brown bag" filled with a little convenient cash for any willing and helpful taker from the broadcast field. So we, the young listeners of the '50s, were being exposed to a new world of sound that was rising up out of studios from Chicago and New York on down through Memphis and New Orleans. It was an odd cultural mix: I would read a chapter of my Bible nightly (managing to read it all the way through over a period of a year or so), then I would slip on my trusty pair of World War II headphones that my cousin Rufus Dodson, an Air Force veteran, had given me. I would then drift away from the spiritual into a fantasy world of music where I would spend the last waking hours of my day. It was not only the sound of the singers, their songs and the instruments, but this new world birthed dreams of freedom and hope for an escape from a simple, confining, and unexciting life. Almost all of us kids of the '40s and '50s, especially the boys, wanted to be cowboys. But times were changing. There was talk of ventures into space and television had brought us new heroes. Soon the Genes and Roys of my childhood would ride off into the sunset. I put my boots in the closet and bought my first pair of rock-'n-roll shoes. The dream was on its way to becoming reality. I didn't even know where "there" was, but I was on my way. Somehow, I felt this music could take me anywhere I wanted to go. And it has. As the great Southern soul music craftsman Dan Penn says, "We couldn't have gone to all those places if we didn't have the music. The only other way guys like us saw the world was in the military." (Dan and his wife, Linda, along with his longtime co-writer, Spooner Oldham, have traveled all over the world doing an acoustic presentation of all their hit songs.) The music has also paid my way to England, France, Germany, Japan, Australia, and other countries I never dreamed I'd see.

It wasn't long before my good friend Aaron Brown and I were in love with the current R&B music of the day. We found out about The Rhythm and Blues Review of 1955 and decided we had to be there. The show was booked into Nashville's Ryman Auditorium by the local legend Abe Stein, who brought many musical events to town. The audience was segregated. In sort of cultural reversal, the whites sat in the usually cheaper and less desirable balcony seats at the tabernacle Captain Ryman built for Christian services in the 1800s. While we whooped and hollered upstairs, the soulful screams and wild applause of the "black folks" drowned us out. The stellar lineup of the top young R&B stars of the day included Big Joe "Shake, Rattle & Roll" Turner, Ruth "Mama, He Treats Your Daughter Mean" Brown, The Clovers (my all-time fave group) singing "One Mint Julip," Lowell Fulsom, The Moonglows featuring Harvey Fuqua (who would later marry into the Barry Gordy, Jr. family and become a top Motown

producer), and The Charms with "Heart of Stone." Naturally, the scantily clad Spence Twins fascinated the teenagers in attendance, including Aaron and me, who got a big kick out of the black lights shining on their fluorescent-painted butts as they pranced across the stage where the usual dance acts were Grand Ole Opry square dancers! It wasn't long until the two Ardee boys were backstage checking out the action. Knowing how energetic and aggressive Aaron is today, I've never pondered on just how we worked our way behind the curtain. For instance, he once told me, "Buzzy, if you carry a clipboard and walk at a fast enough pace, you can get in anywhere!" In a matter of minutes we were drinking screw top wine with The Clovers, who jokingly referred to our crew cut hairdos as Quo Vadis–style cuts.

Joe Turner was particularly nice to us and gave us his autograph. Comedian Al Jackson summed up the spirit of the evening by signing "Be Happy" above his signature on the much treasured souvenir program book. The sight of two scrawny Southern teenagers, who obviously loved their music, must have been unusual for these entertainers who rarely communicated with the white fans in those days. "The bug" bit us that night. We'd never be the same rhythmless white boys again. We had the Beat and we loved it! Soon we were imitating our favorite groups, singing and dancing around Aaron's old four-poster bed, using the posts as microphones and practicing all of the "cool moves" we had seen on that unforgettable night at the Ryman. The dream had been born and I was hooked. Seeing the live performances of what up until then had been voices on the radio was exciting. Being backstage with the entertainers at such a venue had also been special. The world behind the curtain was where I wanted to be.

Dancing to rhythmical blues and early rock-'n-roll records (mostly 78- and 45-rpms) would soon become a reality, thanks to Jay Evans, a young attorney who owned our favorite neighborhood recreation

Review of 1955 Cover

place, Riverwood Riding Academy. For years, my sister, Sally and I rode the rental nags the Academy let young riders take out on the trails bordering our residential area and the Cumberland River. In the early '50s, Jay, who loved teenagers and taught us a lot about horses, would let us have a dance/social on Thursday nights in the small stone-and-pine-paneled clubhouse. There, we first did the bop, a sort of goofy white person's version of a step that evolved from the jitterbug of the '40s. We would play Laverne Baker's "Bop-Ting-a-Ling," Etta James's "Roll with Me Henry," and naturally, some Joe Turner discs. It was also at the Riverwood Clubhouse I saw

Harold Bradley playing guitar for us. He would later become the most recorded musician in Nashville session history. The excitement and energy from that early music not only entertained us and brought out the urge to move to the beat, but for me, planted the idea of performing some of that "good feeling stuff" myself! Aaron and I recently took his four-wheel-drive vehicle up through the Riverwood property and found the old clubhouse in the middle of an overgrown field, deserted, and wasting away, strangely enough, surrounded by housing developments. We had a few laughs as we helped ourselves to a few souvenirs from the scene of much fun from our youth.

My first step on the stage had been at the Belcourt Theatre in Nashville's Hillsboro Village. Ironically where my son Parker now works part time. My mother had encouraged me to audition for *Buffalo Bill*, which was to be a production of the Children's Theatre Company. I won the coveted part of "First Indian" and was soon riding the city bus across town to rehearse and appear in the fun little play. I loved everything about it: the lights, the makeup, the crew, and the fellow actors. Two guys my age, Ira Parker and Willo Collins, were playing the parts of troubadours, playing their guitars and singing. A few years later, we would play in competing rock bands around town. I was impressed by the director, Don Roberts, and admired his gentle and effective creative leadership. Early experiences like this helped to build a desire in me to produce music and visual projects. I will always be grateful that my mother involved my sister and me in activities to expand the cultural experience of our childhood. With the exception of this newfound interest in music, cars, and girls (in that order) were the most exciting things in my life. I would later on, starting in 1968, race sports cars and stocks as a driver in both the amateur and professional ranks. My first financial loss in racing, of which there would be many, was a loan of forty dollars I had saved from my Popsicle route to family friend, Harold Baker as an "investment" in a dirt-track stocker he was building. Harold had promised me a chance to drive the car on tracks around Oak Ridge, Tennessee, where he lived. I never heard from him or my forty bucks again, but I eventually did achieve one of my boyhood dreams of racing by driving various race cars all throughout the U.S. on road courses and city-street events that included the first Detroit Grand Prix, The Meadowlands, Laguna Seca and Riverside in California, Road America and the biggest thrill of all, Daytona.

BUFFALO BILL

by AURAND HARRIS

Cast

First Indian	JIM CASON
Second Indian	JOE SMITH
Beaver Boy	JOE PETERSON
Issac Cody	RAY RUTAN
Bill Cody	JIM MABRY
Singing Star	JUDY SHELLEY
Chief Cut Nose	PRESS MARTIN
Medicine Man	JUDI MENEELY
Yellow Hand	LEWIS AKIN
Mr. Majors	JOHN HOOD
Becky	KELMA WEST
Short One	RONNIE STAUBLY
Fat One	BILLY HODGES
Wild Bill Hickock	JAMES POSTON
First Rider	ROBERT SULLIVAN
First Bandit	ALAN LINDMAN
Second Bandit	JACK MARTIN
Indian Mother	MARY DEE HOLDER

Settlers and Indians . . .

PATRICIA GARDNER	ANNE ROBERTSON
JULIE FRIEDMAN	PATSY HAMILTON
STEPHANIE FITZGERALD	ROBERT SULLIVAN
ELISSA AKIN	SUSAN STILES

Dancers . . .

JOE WHITE	GENE ERICKSEN
JIM CASON	WILLIE HUBBARD
JOE SMITH	TONY BRUSH

Guitar Players .... WILLO COLLINS, IRA PARKER

Prompter .... PATSY HAMILTON

Scenes

The action takes place along the trail to the West. The play is divided into three acts with several scenes in each act.

Credits:

NASHVILLE GAS CO., COVERED WAGON

DANCES, JOY ZIBART

INDIAN DANCES, & COSTUMES,

BOY SCOUTS OF AMERICA

TRYOUTS FOR MR. DOOLEY, JR.
Monday, December 6, 3:30 p.m.

The Nashville Children's Theatre

Presents

BUFFALO BILL

By

AURAND HARRIS

Directed by DON ROBERTS
Technical direction by RAY RUTAN
Settings designed by RAY RUTAN
Costumes executed by MARY ALLEN

(Produced by special arrangement with the Children's Theatre Press, of Anchorage, Kentucky.)

Racing was one way I learned dedication, focus, attitude, and loyalty of friends. In the face of difficult challenges while preparing for a race and outright dangers on the track, as both an amateur or professional driver, I discovered I had to react swiftly and decisively and in as calm a manner as humanly possible. I've attempted to carry these bits of acquired wisdom over into my personal life. Driving competitively on road courses and a few oval tracks was this southern boy's dream come true. More than the cars and the thrill of the speed, I always fondly remember the faithful members of my crew and their families and all the fellow drivers and teams I raced with. From '68 to '88, we crisscrossed the country, racing some of America's great road courses.Terry Tibbott, who crewed for me and encouraged me in my racing throgh those fun days of racing, is still a friend to this day and participates in numerous charitable events our mutual friends are involved in.

Ever since my cousin Barry Barrett had let me drive a neat old '28 Chevrolet, spinning it out in a moss-covered limestone flat-bottom creek out in Rutherford County, I had felt the "need for speed." I spent many wonderful hours of fun on the Barrett Farm near Mona, Tennessee, which in the late '40s did not yet have electrical service or other conveniences. In 1999, Barry turned the property across the road from the old family farm into the beautiful Cedar Crest Golf Club.

When I was thirteen, a change would come about at 1204 Ardee Avenue that forever changed our family. My mother and father got a divorce. My dad was on a fixed income, and like always, finances were tight. I recall my mother telling me in a challenging and prophetic way, "Son, if you're ever going to have anything, you'll have to make it on your own." That meant I would be buying my own car. This was both exciting and scary since it was a new responsibility. In addition to my popsicle route, which Aaron often helped me with for what he claims was a whopping commission of a tenth of my modest profit or worse, I occasionally helped Joe Shanks with what was one of the coolest jobs in the neighborhood, his newspaper route. Saving money was something I learned to do early on and soon I had the $200 to buy a '46 Dodge Sedan from its owner in south Nashville. We would all have lots of fun in that old black monster. Many mornings before school, Aaron or Donald "Duck" Bills would sprint down to my house and help me push the heavy old clunker off. At age fourteen, I was a car owner who could only legally drive to work, school, and church. I had secured one of the best jobs on our side of town, which was riding a Cushman motor scooter, delivering prescription drugs all over Inglewood and East Nashville. Inglewood Pharmacy was owned and operated by the red-faced, high-strung, temper fit–prone Dr. Adams, who called all of us delivery boys "Buster." He would curse us and kick the scooter when we were unable to get it started on a cold winter afternoon. All of us Busters would just laugh behind Doc's back as he fussed and fumed and would go on to our next delivery after he got the scooter running. Except for freezing to death on those wintry rides and getting rear-ended one night in the middle of a busy, rain slicked Gallatin Road, it was a fun job, especially when Aaron and I would hitch a rope to his bike and I'd tow him through the side streets on my route.

Buzz with one of his early race cars,
a Triumph mini-stock at Nashville Fairgrounds Speedway, 1977

In our pre-teen days, we had ridden our beloved bicycles for endless miles around the city, shot BB's at crows, swung on rope swings over the neighborhood creek, rode motorbikes and motorcycles, helmetless, of course, and played football in the Browns' front yard with Aaron's brother, Carl , usually at quarterback. I challenge anyone who claims to have had more fun than we did in those "pre-video game days."

Aaron went on to land the real primo job of the neighborhood, that of sack-and-stock boy at Malone's Market located at the corner of Ardee and Gallatin Road. He is now creator and producer of the A Child's Gift of Lullabyes, an innovative concept that triggered an entire new field of recorded product.

As I struggled through my junior year at Litton High School, little did I know that seated next to me in art class was a young man who would unknowingly change my life. He would open a door for me that would lead to a fascinating career. It would all begin at a tiny television station perched on a hill on Old Hickory Boulevard, just south of Nashville.

Noel Ball, The Casuals, and the Birth of Nashville Rock 'n Roll

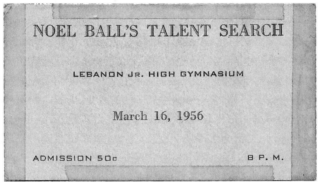

NOEL BALL'S TALENT SEARCH

LEBANON Jr. HIGH GYMNASIUM

March 16, 1956

ADMISSION 50c   8 P. M.

Ticket from first show with the future Casuals, Lebanon,
Tennessee, March 16, 1956

This is my love song, oh darling, for you.
"My Love Song for You"
by Buzz Cason and Richard Williams

The first deejay I ever met had not only a dynamic and charismatic announcing voice, but a similar personality to match his on-air talent. The guys who spun the records in the '50s came in all styles, some "good guys" and some just plain egotistical jerks. The deejay I'm referring to was personable, friendly, and enthusiastic about not only playing records, but also making them. His name was Noel Ball.

Originally from Nebraska, he had come to Nashville in the early '50s to work in local radio at both WMAK and WSIX, both AM outlets. In those days FM was new and had not developed into the powerful medium for music it would soon become. Noel boomed over the airwaves of WSIX, where I met him, with his great radio voice and articulate delivery. He was far superior to most of the competition. However, as a rock-'n-roll jock, he probably overarticulated a little and lacked the zany sense of humor that his contemporaries at the other music city stations had. Some of the competition and fellow microphone mates included Larry Johnson, Wayne "The Brain" Hannah, Roger "Captain Midnight" Schutt, Ralph Emory, and one of the original WKDA "Good Guys," Dick Buckley.

Noel was both an entrepreneur and a television dance show host in addition to being a radio personality. His Saturday afternoon show was appropriately called Saturday Showcase. It was broadcast at the combination studio-tower site of WSIX television, an ABC affiliate owned by a local company. This show gave me my start in music. It began in a left field sort of way, since I couldn't play an instrument and didn't know anything about singing or performing. My public performances had been limited to the church choir and a couple of piano recitals.

Jim Seymore had been in my art class since we were freshmen at Litton High. Being in Annie Ruth Stroud's class was probably the most fun I had at the old high school. There was a unique cast of characters, which numbered about twenty or thirty kids. Among the male students was Bill Taylor, who kept me up-to-date on the happening of a young Elvis Presley, helpful since he had a television and my family did not. Miss Stroud set a high standard for us and constantly referred to the already accomplished upper classmen, Harold Hagewood and Ralph McDonald, two students who would later achieve success in art careers, one as a commercial artist and the other as one of Tennessee's finest wildlife painters. I had sketched and drawn freehand since I was old enough to hold a pencil in my hand and had my sights set on being a commercial artist.

Jim was a goofy sort of guy, very friendly and outgoing and like me, an average artist; a B student, he too was from a broken home. His stepfather was one of the owners of a drive-in theater in nearby Madison where Jim worked on weekends, always providing free hamburgers and cokes to classmates who would come there for weekend movies. There was never a question about the future of Jim, who later went by his middle name, Douglas. His goal was to be in theater or films, hopefully as a director. Although he was a teenager and strictly an amateur at "show business," he showed all the signs of being an affective and successful producer or director. It would be my first encounter with anyone with such ambition, drive, and desire. He wanted to put together a "production" as he referred to it. "Man, why don't you do this Christmas thing I'm doing for television?" Jim asked in class one day. I didn't know what he was talking about, but soon found out he was organizing a pantomime to lip-synch "White Christmas" from the movie of the same name starring Bing Crosby.

"Oh, that's not for me," I told him. But then he offered an incentive that I went for. "There'll be lots of girls," he grinned. "OK, I'll do it," I fired back quickly. Not being a star athlete and basically a bespectacled, pimply-faced eleventh grader, I was anxious to expand my social life. I soon discovered Jim was quite organized in his plans to pull this "number" off at the WSIX studios, where Noel Ball's Saturday Showcase was broadcast live every Saturday. He had choreographed the song and had scheduled several rehearsals to whip the cast into shape. It could have been a classic case of overkill since we soon discovered the standards for the show weren't too lofty. The station needed lots of talent to fill the three or four hours each Saturday afternoon.

Noel Ball hated to turn anyone down. The basic audition requirement to be on his broadcast was to show up! So from miles around they came: tap dancers, fiddlers, square dancers, magicians, musicians, and singers from small communities in Tennessee and Kentucky. The all flocked to Nashville to be seen on the tube. It was a black-and-white world of video then and this wide-eyed Southern boy would soon discover just how powerful this new medium could be. Within two years, The Casuals, and Richard and Buzz would be household names in our area. Noel chomped on cigars, usually unlit, and had a rather devilish twinkle in his eye. To add to the fascination for a teenager like me, he surrounded himself with beautiful girls. A local modeling agency provided several beauties to do commercials and lip-synch the current hits of female recording artists. The pantomime songs were almost always pop or rock tunes. One such young lady was Patsy Willis, who like my future band mates, had attended East Nashville High School. She became Noel's assistant and later wrote a few songs when he moved on into producing records. The attractive, dark-skinned brunette was personable and very supportive of much of the young talent on the show.

At the foot of the station's tower was the cramped-up studio where all the broadcasting was done, including all the news, sports and even live wrestling on Saturday nights. It was a new world for me—the lights, the cameras (only two at the time), and the friendly crew, including the funny and always helpful cameraman Norm Frasier, confirmed my new belief that this was the place for me.

The production number went over well. We made some new friends and were truly bitten by the showbiz bug. Soon, Jim and I had hung around on Saturdays long enough to work our way into a set designing and painting job. We did a few backdrops for Noel and the station paid us forty dollars a job. We were in business! One night after a show, the two excited new "professionals" had a serious scare heading home from the hill. We were making a rain-slicked turn on Granny White Pike just adjacent to David Lipscomb College. Jim's mom had restored an old round top '41 Plymouth for him to drive—painted in robin's egg blue. We had packed it with our painting supplies, schoolbooks, and assorted junk. Jim was not a particularly good driver. His zany personality carried over to his driving habits. Already being an aspiring sports car driver, having learned about Ferraris and about races like the Le Mans and the Mille Miglia from my fellow Boy Scout Bobby Manlove, I was aware of the body roll feeling of a car being overcorrected by an overreactive driver, as we used to speed around Inglewood in his little Nash Rambler pretending we were on a great road course.

On that night in '56, I shouted, "Look out! She's going to roll! Hold on!" Jim, still laughing, frantically let go of the wheel and reached up to brace himself on the headliner of the Plymouth. And roll she did! Not a full one, but up on the top in the middle of Granny White Pike, nearly missing a small guardrail, which overlooked a creek below. Books, paint cans, lunchboxes, and other tools all came raining down on us! We wound up freely floundering about in the Plymouth, which in those days had no seatbelts or harnesses. Cars were built so tough then that we turned the car over, managed to get it started and drove on back to Inglewood. After that, Jim had the only car in the school parking lot with a slightly modified (as in bashed-in) roof. After graduation, Jim moved to L.A. I heard from him a few times, then later on lost touch with him. I remain grateful to Jim Seymore for giving me my first break and opportunity to begin living a professional life in a business I have truly enjoyed.

Richard Williams and His Trio was Richard on piano and vocals, Johnny McCreery on guitar, Chester Power on accordion, and Billy Smith on drums. By the time these East High students began making semi-regular appearances on Saturday Showcase, I had been elevated to a solo performer status. I lip-synched current R&B hits. Many times performing the songs of the Moonglows, "Sincerely" aping Harvey Fuqua's lead vocal part, Otis Williams of The Charms with "Hearts of Stone," and other black artists. I would sometimes enlist buddies, including such "hood"-like characters Gene McElweay and Casey Jones, to perform with me under the fictitious group name The Manhattans, long before the legit group of that name was founded.

To my R&B ears, Richard and the band really played white. Once, however, I heard their live sound I knew I had to sing and not lip-synch anymore. How I was going to get to that point I didn't know. I wanted to sing the black stuff not the white Pat Boone covers they were doing. The artists I was into by then included B.B. King, James Brown & the Famous Flames, Chuck Berry, Ray Charles, and anyone else on the bright orange Atlantic Label.

Somewhere along the way Richard had acquired a manager of sorts. He was Gerald Pinkelton, who also used the show name "Jerry King." Jerry had been trained by the legendary and notorious Vernon Way, who booked small schools around the state and sold sponsors at ten dollars each to local businessmen. He usually kept that money himself and whatever he collected at the gate, leaving the entertainers mainly playing for experience. The story goes that Vernon hustled every female singer who appeared on one of his shows. He was also credited with the line, "Girl, don't you ever eat at home?" when either one of his dates or a female singer might suggest having a meal after a show. With Jerry's help we would later pick up on Vernon's techniques for promoting a show, especially selling sponsors. The idea was to sell the banker in a small town first, and the other business in the community would follow. I recall one incident in Lafayette, Tennessee, when Billy Smith and I were visiting with a lady who was the president of the bank: after hearing our pitch, she said, "Boys, why don't you go home and get a job?" Billy and I never sold sponsors again.

Noel Ball received lots of mail. Many of the schools, mainly in rural areas, would request that Noel bring his talent search to their school. We, as regular entertainers on the TV show, received mail also and were sometimes asked to appear. One particular night, Noel and I flew in a four-seat aircraft to Murfreesboro, only thirty miles down the road, which was two lanes in those days. We probably saved about a half hour by flying. We had done a show at a local Nashville high school beauty contest. So, we were double-booked that night. Noel, an aspiring pilot himself, decided we could make both gigs if we flew. That particular night, in order to make the show, Noel lured a more experienced pilot and we took off on a pitch-black night. We landed to the glow of about twenty or so cars lighting up the little airstrip with their headlights. A risky adventure, but fear didn't always figure in when a show was at stake.

I continued to have fun pantomiming to those old 45s and 78-rpm records, but I still longed to sing. I had been pestering Jerry into talking the band into letting me perform with them.

He'd say, "Hell, you can't sing!"

I asked, "How do you know?" And of course I didn't know myself. Little did I realize his wife, Betty, knew of my desire to grab the microphone and had been urging Jerry to let me sing. "Let Buzzy sing," she would demand.

So, finally he gave in and said I could do a song at an upcoming Noel Ball live show. "Look! Richard's the singer but you can have a chance. Just leave those damn records at home and you'll have to sing!" It sounded like a plan to me. So, I showed up at the next show empty-handed. Our next booking just happened to be in my father's hometown.

On March 16, 1956, at the Lebanon High School in Wilson County, Tennessee, Richard asked, "What song do you know?" when he learned I was to sing.

"'Blue Suede Shoes' in C, I think," I replied. All the guys were nice to me and we worked up the Carl Perkins hit. I nervously anticipated my spot on the show. Then Jerry introduced me. It went over well. By then screaming girls and enthusiastic rock-'n-roll fans were in vogue. I loved it! The band seemed to accept me. "Can we do this again?" I asked. "Why not?" Richard smiled. I had earned my way in. We began booking the Jerry King Rock 'n Roll Show, featuring Richard Williams and His Trio and at the bottom of the bill, just above "many others" was Buzz and Richard.

This shot reflects the joy of rock 'n roll, from backstage at the Donelson Theatre.

One afternoon, Richard came over to my house on Ardee and we wrote our first song. I knew very few chords on the piano and none on the guitar. So, Richard's help with our first song, "My Love Song for You," was greatly appreciated. The song was in the key of C to A Minor, F, G chord progression that was so predominant in the R&B ballads of the day. That old upright piano in the tiny living room on Ardee Avenue had never sounded so good. The birth of a song is a magical and spiritual occurrence in our creative world and I felt a new spark of positive energy flow through me when we sang the song through for the first time that day.

I thought it would be cool to name the band. So after submitting the "Casuals" to the group at our next rehearsal, we were officially an organized band. Billy was always recognized as the business manager and leader of the band, and Richard and I usually picked out the songs we performed. As for selling sponsors we were quite successful until that Lafayette, Tennessee, incident. We always promised the sponsors we would put their name on the poster for the upcoming show.

So under Jerry's supervision we would sneak into Hatch Show Print, to print our posters at night. Using our own wooden blocks with our likeness on them, we would moonlight and turn out enough posters for our upcoming gigs, which were usually booked at schools and small indoor and drive-in theaters in our area.

Another rather innocent scam we occasionally attempted was to get that coveted free meal. I remember one time we were headed for a school somewhere near Centerville, Tennessee.

Jerry said, "This looks good. Pull over here." We had driven up a dusty driveway to a beautiful little frame house and it was just about dinnertime. Jerry knocked on the door with a couple of us in our sport coats politely standing behind him.

"Does Mrs. Cason live here?" he asked.

"Why, no," the little lady replied. "This is the Smith residence."

Jerry frowned, shook his head, and sadly explained, "These boys are on their way to play a benefit show for the school up the road and we were supposed to stop on the way and have dinner with these folks, the Casons."

"Oh my," Mrs. Smith said. "You boys must be hungry. I don't know no Casons, but you can sure come in and eat with us tonight." It was a fun trick that worked for us. And since we were only making two or three dollars each per show, eating out was a rarity.

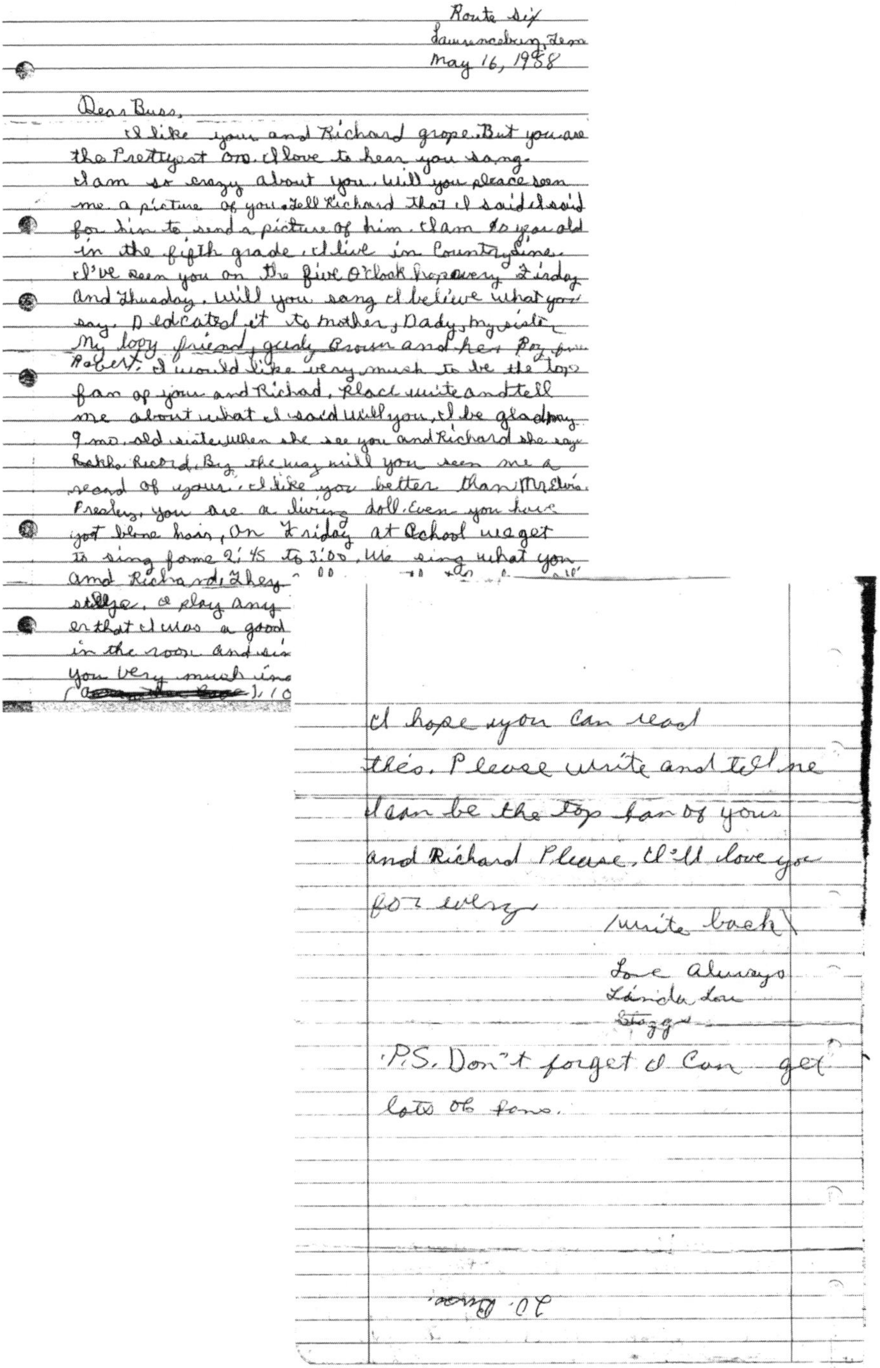

Route Six
Summersburg, Tenn
May 16, 1958

Dear Buss,

I like you and Richard grope. But you are the prettyest oro. I love to hear you sang. I am so crazy about you. Will you please soon me a picture of you. Tell Richard that I said I said for him to send a picture of him. I am 10 years old in the fifth grade. I live in County Line. I've seen you on the five O'clock hop every Tuesday and Thursday. Will you sang I believe what you say. I dedicated it to mother, Dady, my sister My loyy friend, Judy Brown and her Boy friend Robert. I would like very much to be the top fan of you and Richard. Plact write and tell me about what I said will you. I be glad, my 9 mo. old sister when she see you and Richard she say Rahh. Record. By the way will you seen me a reord of yours. I like you better than Mr Elvis. Presley. you are a living doll. even you have got blone hair. On Friday at school we get to sing from 2:45 to 3:00. We sing what you and Richard. They still ye. I play any er that I was a good in the room and sis you very much in ( ), 10

I hope you can read this. Please write and tell me I can be the top fan of yours and Richard Please. I'll love you for evey.

write back

Love always
Linda Lou
Stizgs

P.S. Don't forget I Can get lots of fans.

J.D. Brow.

A fan letter from one of our Five O'Clcok Hop fans.

The Casuals' popularity increased in the Nashville area, not only due to our now occasional appearances on Noel's show and regular spots on Dave Overton's Five O'Clock Hop, a dance show on Channel 5, but also due to the fact that we played anywhere you could plug in, as we would laughingly boast. Quite possibly, the first real taste of the spirit and energy of live rock 'n roll came when we appeared on Noel's variety show at the Donelson Theatre, on the outskirts of Nashville.

For the first time, we heard our first screams from young fans there and signed autographs in the crowded backstage area and in the parking lot. It is understandable how teenagers like we were or those in their early twenties could see life in an unrealistic or jaded way while receiving such adulation and admiration. Although it was on a local scale, we suddenly felt like we were on the way to "being somebody" in this new and exciting world of rock 'n roll. And guess what? We had fan letters to prove our popularity!

The band would soon be named The Casuals.

The Beatles had the Cavern, Elvis Presley the Louisiana Hayride, and The Casuals had a small neighborhood theater, located just a stone's throw away from the Hermitage, home of Andrew Jackson, seventh president of the United States. The reaction to our crude and basic style of rock, the acceptance of our own songs, and the sheer thrill of how the music and our moves on stage excited the kids were unlike anything we had ever experienced. We learned in just a few appearances just how valuable and important it was to be showmen. We experimented and tried out new routines on each show, always reinventing the ones that seemed to work every time.

In time, however, I have learned that spontaneity and improvisation are as key to the success of a show as a well-planned set list of well-rehearsed numbers.

In the same way audiences dance freestyle at their seats or in the aisles, the entertainer is more often than not being impulsively motivated by the music to dance and move about the stage in a way that pleases and excites the crowd.

As The Casuals, we found the end result of driving home a rousing, up-tempo song could work the crowd into a frenzy. No true rocker has ever been ashamed of enticing the fans to rush the stage or scream for more at the end of a set. It's as if "leave them wanting more" is the creed of a successful entertainer and the art of knowing exactly when to leave the stage is equally important. From the landmark Donelson Theatre venue we soon moved to playing the roofs of concession stands. In addition to concession stands at drive-in theaters, we played parking lots, skating rinks, small night clubs (which were rare), and the soon-to-be lucrative fraternity parties circuit. Kappa Sig at Vanderbilt University was our first frat party dance and it led to many more on that campus as well as Sewanee, Alabama, and others. In keeping with the East Nashville tradition, Jimmy Stein, another Inglewood boy, booked us on that first Vandy gig. We had to adjust to the close quarters of the fraternity house basements, where we had to perform. We had gained recognition around town, not only by the music we played and the fact that we appeared on a local television show, but that we put on a hard rockin' show—we jumped around, danced, and worked the crowd and generally had a good time. Some of the students, the guys in particular, got quite drunk and created havoc at the parties. It was funny and a little frightening in that I got into a pushing and shoving bout with the same guy at one of the fraternities two times one year apart. He kept trying to grab the microphone and I would not let him have it. Also, I still have a vision of our guitar player, Wayne Moss, perched on his Fender amp to avoid standing in the beer and booze that covered the floor.

The music of the late '50s was becoming more exciting each week as stacks of brightly labeled 45-rpm vinyl records arrived at radio stations and in the record stores, which were largely mom-and-pop outlets or in the department-store record shelves. The anticipation of the next Elvis record was likened unto the excitement of waiting on a new Beatles release later on in the '60s. As the volume and the popularity of the new music increased, our repertoire also grew rapidly. We resented the watered-down covers of such R&B hits as Pat Boone's "Tutti Frutti" and "Long Tall Sally," both written and recorded by Little Richard. The Diamonds also murdered "Hearts of Stone," the song cut originally by the great Otis Williams and The Charms. I guess we fancied ourselves as purists when it came to R&B music, so we strived to perform the songs as closely as we could to the original versions. The one song that brought us more recognition on the local party circuit was "Bo Diddley," which of course, was the trademark of Bo himself. As the guitarist ground away at the tremeloed one-chord chant, Bill Smith would move away from his drum kit and I would drag the floor tom all over the dance floor as the band and crowd screamed along, "Hey Bo Diddley." Bo could outdraw almost any entertainer in several cities in the South, including Nashville. We would play his theme song for at least ten minutes at a time on many occasions. We had written very few originals in those early days, so we sang from the catalogues of Gene Vincent, Carl Perkins, Big Joe Turner, Jimmy Reed, Jerry Lee, The Clovers, The Moonglows, and Eddie Cochran. The latter we would go on to back up in Kansas City and St. Louis, Missouri. And had Eddie not met an untimely death, he would have become one of rock's super-stars. Two of Eddie's rockers, "Summertime Blues" and "C'mon Everybody," have become true classics.

Another fun story associated with the first recording I made with The Casuals in 1957. Richard and I told Noel about the song we had written. He was excited and told us he had been thinking about moonlighting a recording session in the WSIX studios after midnight one evening following his radio show. Back then, nearly all the radio stations had studios for live music. As a kid I had heard country shows broadcast from the very room we would be attempting to cut our first "disc" in. Whether Noel could recognize a hit when he heard it, I don't know, but when we played "My Love Song for You" for him, he sure made us feel like we had a winner on our hands.

"We'll just have to be cool about it. ['Cool' meaning coy or clever, keeping it quiet about our session.] The old man wouldn't like it," Noel declared, referring to Louis Draughon, the manager of WSIX, one of the city's first AM radio stations. Never to be one exactly on the "up and up" in business dealings, it didn't surprise us that Noel would do something a little shady. But of course, being desperate to make a recording ourselves, we were willing to take whatever chances were required to hear ourselves on the radio.

As was our usual routine, we rehearsed at both Billy Smith's in Inglewood or at Richard's on Joseph Avenue, further down in East Nashville. I always thought it ironic that my first vocal partner and I came from the very same street in the lower-middle class section of our city. The band worked up "My Love Song for You" and "Help Me," also written with Richard, which would be our first single recording. The A-side was an R&B ballad of sorts and "Help Me" was a thrown together tune with a slightly quicker tempo, kind of blues-like. Basically we were inept at playing any kind of session music. Johnny McCreery and I had cut a two-song demo of "Blue Suede Shoes" and "Heartbreak Hotel" at the old Reavis Studio on Broadway and that was the extent of our recording experience. Johnny was the first guitarist to show me open chords and the "G-boogie," which I rehearsed nightly on my newly purchased Harmony guitar. With Johnny on guitar; Chester Power on piano; Bill Smith on drums; a guest player, Wayne Pilkinton; Clarence Wittenmier, who played with us occasionally on sax; and Richard and me on vocals—we recorded the two songs on quarter-inch monaural tape and used 71/2-ips "slapback tape" for reverb or echo for the songs. We were thrilled hearing ourselves as a band for the first time on tape. It was not only a kick but a little scary. There was no fixing mistakes on a monaural or one-track tape, no overdubs or punch-ins as we do today. With the advent of digital recording we can now move notes and instrumental passages around the song as desired. None of that was possible on that old Ampex 350 machine, so we accepted the first take out of the lot and went with it. Editing in those days was done with a razor blade!

Noel was in the process of starting an independent record company with local businessman Buzz Wilburn, who would later have a long and successful career with Capitol Records in Los Angeles. They called the label Nu-Sound. I designed a logo for the label with pen and ink and since Buzz was associated with a printing company, he gave his new company a break on printing the labels, which featured my rather crude drawing in silver on a dark green background. Of course, to all of us Casuals it looked great! We soon had records in our hand. When Noel dropped the needle on that 45-rpm single on WSIX and we heard it on the air for the first time, it was a feeling I would never forget. It's still awesome to hear a new song you either have written or produced being played on radio or seeing a video of a song for the first time.

In the '50s, downtown Nashville's 3rd Avenue was a bustling mix of retail shops and small businesses. At my mother's urging, I took over Billy Jones's job at one of the shops along 3rd, McNellis Letter Service. My Saturday morning assignment was to print a local church program for the service the next day. The equipment we used was an old-style, then state-of-the-art mimeograph machine. I would usually hitch-hike to town to work from about nine to twelve, make my fifty cents an hour and spend twenty-five cents on a burger and Coke at the Corner Cafe. Walking out of that greasy spoon with my clothes all smoked up and smelly, I had no idea that a much more interesting place of business existed just a block away and how it would play a part in my career in '57.

*"My Love Song for You" performed by The Casuals, written by Buzz and Richard Williams,
Nu-sound label, designed by Buzz*

By the time that first record was released, my trips to Ernie's Record Mart on 3rd Avenue became more exciting than before when I was picking up records to panto-mime. Besides the fact that "Happy Jack," whose real name was Morgan Babb, did his morning radio show from the storefront, I was checking on sales of the new Casuals record. Perched up in a small display area in the front window of Ernie's, Morgan cut a striking and memorable figure. Morgan's morning drive show for WSOK (presently WVOL) was the first remote radio show I ever witnessed. His warm and friendly personality was enhanced by his energetic delivery. "Wake up and live," "get up and give," "when you're snoozin' you're losin,' so let's get movin'!"he would bark out before playing one of the hot R&B records of the day. I was always keen to hear what records he black jocks were playing, especially knowing those songs would most likely be in our show sets soon. Starting with the first song I ever had released, I have always enjoyed visiting and contacting radio station folks. Many of the disc jockeys and music directors I met at smaller stations went on to larger markets and have remained friends through the years.

To keep up with the up and coming single records, I'd talk to soft spoken, friendly, cigar-chewing Jimmy Lancaster, who managed Ernie's, and would mutter something like, "It's a pretty good number, it's selling a few," which meant a song was likely to be a hit! " Many of these rocking songs would become part of our show."I'm sellin' a few of that Casuals record too!,"he would add. Ernie's would also be where I first met blues-loving Mac Gayden, who would later become a great friend and co-writer. We were selling a few copies, so Noel got in touch with Randy Wood, who owned Dot Records, and convinced him to pick up the new record for his hot new label. We soon saw those same two songs on the multicolored Dot label. We thought we were on our way as recording stars! And as far as local success we already were. Our song was soon in the local Top 10 at WSIX, WMAK, and the local Top 40 station WKDA. The advent of the "combo" party had hit the more wealthy sections of our city and we were soon the hot act to book for your frat, sorority, or prom. Our calendars were filling up; we quit our part-time jobs and were seriously considering a full-time musical career. The summer of '57 was a landmark time for us. It all began when The Everly Brothers hit with the Boudleaux and Felice Bryant song "Bye Bye Love."

For us it was "Bye Bye Nashville" and on to a new phase of our lives we had longed to travel: "The Road."

The Road

Another flat on Elizabeth, the Caddy

In the beginning it wasn't nothing like it is today
Played the little lounges didn't have no big halls to play
Old shoddy buses or station wagons got 'em to their gigs
Never imagined this thing would ever get this big.

"In the Beginning (A Sign of the Times)"
by Buzz Cason and Austin Roberts

Richard Williams was a hustler. Not only was he a great rock-'n-roll singer and piano player, but he could always scare up bookings for our band, The Casuals, which he had started and continued to lead for years after most of us original members had moved on. He was a public relations guy of sorts and always had his feelers out for a possible gig, which ranged between $125 and $250 per night for our group. In those days, the $125 was more likely the fee.

Before the advent of Music Row, much of the music business centered around a few blocks of 7th Avenue North in downtown Nashville. Next to the Clarkston Hotel where many musicians hung out and drank coffee was the Elk's hall. It housed several offices including Jack Stapp and Buddy Killen's Tree Music, which would become a highly successful publishing company and later be sold to Sony. I recall Buddy yelling at me from his office door, "Hey, I was supposed to have that song you wrote!" referring to the publishing rights to a song, "Til You Come Back to Me," which I had written with Jeff Daniels, a writer Buddy knew. The song was released as a B-side of our second release on Dot, "Hello Love." I had given the song to Gallatin Music, owned by Randy Wood, not knowing Jeff had promised it to Buddy. Back then, publishers very seldom co-published with each other. Although the song never made much money and wasn't a hit, it took years for Buddy to quit reminding me that he didn't get the song. It had been written in a cheap hotel room in our first tour in '57.

The Casuals 1957 - The Birth of Nashville Rock 'n Roll

The way we fell into that road trip was by chance and was due to perfect timing on Richard's part. He would hit the booking offices looking for work for the band. "I've got a band with two singers,!" Richard fired back after a secretary at the John Kelly Agency told him, "We need a rock-'n-roll band to replace The Everly Brothers this summer."

"We can do that," he told the beautiful girl, whom we later discovered was country singer and rodeo queen Judy Lynn, who was married to John Kelly, the owner of the agency. Judy was to sing on the tour also. Mr. Kelly had a son from a previous marriage, rockabilly singer Pat Shannon, who would also appear on the sixty-day string of county fair dates. Pat wasn't much of a singer, but dressed flashy and put on a good show. Lucky for us he didn't have much of an ear for music because when he heard us he thought we were good enough for the tour.

We weren't very accomplished at singing or playing yet. He seemed to click with us although we later discovered his erratic and irrational behavior combined with his reckless driving habits would lead to arguments and even fights. One day, Chester and Pat had a good bout in a hot, dusty cattle pen in the plains of Oklahoma, and as expected, no one won. Chester and I would sometime ride with Pat in his fast black '57 Dodge; they bugged each other constantly, and scuffles resulted, but no one was ever hurt badly. They were both lousy fighters.

I guess it was an hour of desperation that Mr. Kelly hired us, and since we were still Nashville's first and only rock band, we were definitely in the right place at the right time. We worked for the small fee he was offering and didn't care; we just wanted to hit the road! We had heard about all the fun you had on tour, the new places you would see, the new faces you'd meet, the radio people, and the stars that varied from show to show. Just a few days after my graduation I was preparing for the trip, excitedly packing the bass drum into the backseat of Chester's '55 Chevy and stuffing the luggage into the carrier strapped to the top of the bright yellow sedan. Our inexperience raised its head early when we discovered after the first day out that we didn't have enough room for us and all our stuff. We needed a trailer. We also found out Chester had installed a governor on the carburetor, preventing the car from going over 55 mph. We couldn't pass anyone! I thought we'd never get across Arkansas on the way to our first show in Oklahoma. A couple of us hitched rides with other members of the show.

"Hawk!" Tommy Williams screamed as he hit the brakes of his powerful new V8-equipped Pontiac coupe. I was riding with Tommy, who was playing fiddle and guitar on the tour. He traveled with a .22-caliber rifle with a scope mounted on his dash. Fortunately for us, there were very few troopers on those remote roads at the time. He would either hand it over to me or take a shot himself at the unsuspecting wildlife.

I kept telling him, "Man, we ought to shoot buzzards instead of those pretty hawks." Tommy just enjoyed shooting, hoping to break up the boredom of the long drives, which were sometimes as much as five to seven hundred miles a day. We seldom killed anything, and we did manage to make it to that first show of that long, hot summer in Broken Bow, Oklahoma, a tiny town with a typical Western main street located just across the Arkansas-Oklahoma line in Indian territory, surrounded by reservations. Just checking into the only hotel in town was an adventure since we had little travel experience. While Richard handled the registration, we clowned around outside, happy to be out of the cars. I snapped a photo of Mel Tillis, a wet-behind-the-ears singer who was poking his head out of the window of his room. He was wearing a little Ben Hogan–style golf cap he'd borrowed from me and was stuttering craziness down on us.

Mel had moved up from Florida and would go on to become a great writer-performer. It thrilled me in the early '80s when he had a Top 5 hit with "A Million Old Goodbyes," which I co-wrote with Bobby Russell and Steve Gibb. Mel would later become one of country music's highly successful songwriters and recording artists.

Johnny and Jack and Kitty Wells were very popular in country music and were headlining that first show. I don't think they knew exactly what to think about us. We were not country. My first song on the road was "That'll Be the Day," the smash hit by Buddy Holly & the Crickets. We played on a flatbed trailer that night, but as far as I was concerned, it was as grand as Carnegie Hall or the Hollywood Bowl. We had arrived, for sure. It was a little strange for us to play on a stage lined with hay bales, but we paid little attention to the setting since we were having fun and our show was going over so well. Minnie Pearl was on the bill as well. It was my first time meeting her and her husband, Henry Cannon, who was also her pilot.

She came up to me as asked, "What in the world are you doing out here?"

"Well, we're on the tour, ma'am," I proudly answered.

"What about your education? Aren't you going to college?" she demanded. I told her how I planned to turn down a scholarship to go to Peabody College in Nashville and study art that coming fall to pursue music full time.

She got in my face immediately with "You get yourself back home and get back in school. This business will wait on you." Of course, I didn't listen to her. I haven't been back to school (yet) and I never looked back.

A few years later and after the good fortune of a few hit songs,I was able to purchase a house on Curtiswood lane, on property which bordered the Governors Mansion in and was next door to country star, Webb Pierce and accross the road from the phenominal Ray Stevens. Ray, the successful multi-talented artist and a friend of mine and Webb, whom iI had sung behind on the road, had an ongoing battle over Webb's fans in their tour buses blocking our street on Saturday mornings. After a few confrontations, Webb, rather seriously told the press, "That's what he gets for movin' across the street from a star!"

Minnie and Henry lived on Glen Leven Drive, which was also close to our home. Minnie, who had no children of her own, loved to invite the neighborhood kids, which included our daughter Tammy, to swim in her pool. On one such occasion, I kidded her by reminding her about her advice to me that night back in Oklahoma. I told her, "Minnie, who knows, if I had listened to you, I might not have stayed in the music business or be living close to you in this nice neighborhood." " I'd probably be back in Inglewood pumpin' gas!"

Tommy Williams had given our show a professional touch. It took a "summit meeting" in Iowa to bring about a change in our musical lineup. "This is the worst "shew" I've ever had on the road!" John Kelly shouted in his unusual dialect. He had called us all together in a Cedar Rapids, Iowa, hotel conference room to tell us we had to have a more country-sounding band or we would be going home. "What this "shew" needs is a fiddle," he added.

"What had this tour come to?" I thought to myself as we all tried to hide our laughter. Had we sold out? When we took the tour, we thought we would be playing our own rock stuff in addition to backing Pat on his rockabilly and Judy's Western tunes. As it turned out, the office in Nashville was receiving calls from some of the county fairs that we were rockin' a little too much. But, a fiddle? We had never seen one up close much less had one in the band. With Tommy's guidance, we learned some real country, real quick. We wanted to finish that tour and with Tommy's help and talent, we did.

Our original guitarist, Johnny McCreery, didn't last long on the road and went into the insurance business and later into radio, where he became a successful broadcaster and station owner. Enter Tommy once more. In addition to fiddle, he also played good lead guitar, filling in until we hired another Tommy from Missouri. Tommy Sykes played a hot Fender Telecaster, jumped around all over the stage and wore his hair in a flattop style. He was a great guy and easy to work with. We thought he would be with the band indefinitely until he asked for a day off to make a quick trip home to Missouri to see his family. He was to rejoin the show, but never came back.

About twenty-five years later, he called my office. I recognized the name immediately when my assistant told me of his call and I surprised him by screaming, "Man, we're still waitin' for you, where are you?"

With his quick wit, he jumped back with, "I'll be there man, trust me!" He had caught Mel Tillis's attention on the fair tour and later on Mel hired him, and he was with Mel's Statesiders band for several years.

In addition to backing Pat, we also backed other artists, including Jeff Daniels, the second guy I would attempt to co-write with. Jeff had "the swagger." He was a cocky guy with slicked-back black hair and a tanned face that featured an interesting wandering eye. His warm personality and bright smile overcame any problems he might have communicating with anyone in his lower Alabama twang. He constantly jabbered about Mobile and his mentor radio cowboy, Jack Cardwell. He had recorded a few rockabilly sides for Hickory Records and had acquired an Elvis complex, convincing us he definitely thought he was the "Memphis Cat" himself at times, especially when he was on stage, and with his white sport coat, shiny black shirt, tight-fitting black pants, and white loafers he was "ready," as the country boys used to say, as he shook and jumped around frantically. It was so amusing for us to observe his quirky habits, which included mailing home a money order at least every other day and requiring us younger guys to learn the art of yelling at ladies of any age whom our car would pass by in the small Midwest towns we were appearing in. "Hey Mamar!" (his pronunciation of Mamas) was to be shouted at any female we drove by regardless of the time of day or what the weather was. Rain or shine, the windows were to be rolled down and the ladies were to be properly addressed in the

Jeff Daniels style. He was quite a character, and after that rather grueling tour, I understand he settled down in Mobile and became an evangelical preacher, writing a few songs occasionally under his real name, Luke McDaniel.

We were playing a fair somewhere in Illinois, and as usual, the stage was set up in the infield of a dirt racetrack that served as turf for both horses and cars to race. To add to our country repertoire I had started doing an Ernest Tubb imitation of "Walkin' the Floor over You." The number required a cowboy hat, which I had lost the night before. Not realizing the hat wasn't in our props box until the show had already started, I had to make a mad dash in my show outfit across the track to the Midway to buy a cheap straw hat for our act. I found the hat easily, but I only had one song to buy it and get back on stage. I ran into a problem when I tried to get back in the stage area. Several older retired gentlemen were working security at the gate I desperately needed to get through. One of them in particular decided has was not going to let me back in the infield.

"You don't have a pass," he yelled as I waved the hat and assured him I was on the show.

"Sir, do you think I'd be wearing this crazy turquoise-colored wool sport coat in this heat if I weren't on the show?" I shouted back, trying still to respect my elders. He said he didn't care what I had on, I wasn't going through that gate. I did not see his walking cane as I charged past him, but I did "see stars" when he caught me in the head with one blow and the mouth with another using that cane. By then a real nice man who played the rear end of a horse in a comedy act on our show intervened and stopped the old fellow from beating me even sillier than I was. George and his wife, who played the more desirable front end of the horse, were from Chicago's Midwest Jamboree and had seen it all around those fairs, so he told the man he'd have him arrested and rushed me off to the stage where I arrived in time to do Ernest.

When I hit the stage, Richard held the microphone to his side and said, "Man, you're bleeding!" I wiped off my mouth and we went on with the show. Later on we had lots of laughs about the incident.

The pace was hectic, the pay was slim, and we stayed and dined in the cheapest places we could find. But, it was OK. We were seeing Middle America and we were officially a traveling band with dreams of playing the big auditoriums and hopes of either headlining or backing a major artist when our long, hot summer trek was finished. The girls were still screaming, we had a new station wagon, and our music was getting better every night. Could being in school or working a nine-to-five back home be better than that? We never slowed down long enough to know. It was, "What town is next?" We wound up that frantic, hot, but exhilarating string of fair dates throughout the Midwest and came back to Middle Tennessee, seeking whatever work we could find, playing National Guard Armories, theatres, and private parties.

At one point in 1958, we were recommended to Dub Allbritten, who managed Brenda Lee, by Oscar Davis, a sharp dressed manager and booking agent, who managed Jerry Lee Lewis and liked our band. "You need to hear these kids," Oscar advised Dub. So with the idea in mind of a teenage band backing his even younger up and coming star, Dub asked us to trek up to Rockford, Illinois at the City Audtorium there to audition in the afternoon for Brenda and if it went well, play the show that night. We clicked instantly. Brenda and Dub liked us and thus began a long relationship between Brenda and the Casuals. She simply stood there, snapping her fingers and wailing away wth that powerful voice, in a style that embraced rock, gospel as well as country. We were blown away with Brenda's voice and showmanship, even though we had to place a chair in front of the old style footlights so the crowd could see her. She would become the Taylor Swift of her day, outselling all other female artists of the early sixties.

One night after playing in Mississippi, we crossed the state line into Alabama and stopped at Rogers Truck Stop, not far from Vernon to get a late night snack and coffee. A young man, who seemed a little younger than us, was over by the Seeburg juke box selecting some tunes. One song he played was a new one by Conway Twitty, who was just beginning to record hits for the MGM label. The youngster seeing our shiny new '61 black Chevy Impala station wagon pulling a matching trailer, had thought to himself. "now that's a band." So the curious, slim kid, rather shyly strolled over to our table and greeted us. As he tells it, I jumped up and stuck out my hand telling him, "Hi, I'm Buzz Cason, we're the Casuals we just came from Columbus Mississippi and we back up Brenda Lee!" He replied smiling, "I'm Dan Penn and I wrote "Is A Bluebird Blue!"I later told Dan that later on down the road tht night ,we all had a good laugh when I told the boys, "That fool thinks he wrote "Is A Bluebird Blue Bird Blue!" Of course later on we found out that he had written the song and like so many multitudes of music fans around the world came to respect and love this true southern musical treasure of a man.

I was always looking for session work as a singer and continually working on my songwriting. On many occasions, disc jockeys booked us at record hops for a percentage of the gate proceeds.

One of the top deejays in our area was Hugh "Baby" Jarrett, a former bass singer with The Jordanaires. Hugh loved The Casuals, especially Richard and me. He got the not-so-shabby idea of forming a new vocal group to compete with his former group and the Anita Kerr Singers, two ensembles of background singers who did the majority of the voices for all the sessions in Nashville. Hugh recruited Marijohn Wilkin to not only sing with us on sessions, but to assist in training Richard and me to read charts and execute the proper intervals and tones necessary to produce a smooth, blended sound. Marijohn was also a successful songwriter and would later have her country song "Long Black Veil," co-written with Danny Dill, cut by Mick Jagger, and "I Just Don't Understand," co-written with Kent Westbury, cut by The Beatles. We wound up getting a fair amount of work when we were in town and not on the road. It was frustrating for us because we usually made more on two sessions than we made all week with the band.

Another pivotal point in my career also came courtesy of Hugh Jarrett: he convinced his old friend Al Bennett to sign us to his record label, Liberty Records, located in Hollywood. We aptly named the group, The Statues. Al sent none other than Thomas "Snuff" Garrett in to produce us. Hearing his name, we expected an old man, but he turned out to be just a couple years older than Richard and me. Our first record, a version of The Clovers' "Blue Velvet" hit the bottom of the charts and sold a few copies. Not long after that, Snuff called to inform me we needed to do a cover record of a song that was causing a stir because the song "Look For A Star" was in a popular low-budget horror film called Circus of Horrors. I was excited until I heard the soundtrack cut of the song. I didn't much care for it, but it sounded commercial. I learned it on a Friday; we cut it on a Saturday; and because Liberty had strong connections at the L.A. pressing plant, my record hit the streets and was shipped to stations and distributors on Monday!

As I left the studio, Snuff asked Sy Waronker, who flew in for the session, "What are we gonna call Buzzer on this record?"

Sy asked back, "What's the other kid's name?"

Snuff answered, "Gary Mills, Sy."

"Screw it, we'll call him Garry Miles!" Sy announced. So here I was, with a song I barely knew on the radio almost overnight covering not only another artist's song, but his name too! Can you imagine the lawsuits that would result from a record company pulling a stunt like that nowadays? Well, at least I had two r's in Garry. In a roundabout way, my dream of having a hit record as an artist had come true, not knowing the bubble would quickly burst, and I would never have another hit single as Garry Miles.

I made a few extra bucks on the road as Garry and I remained in the band wearing my glasses and a tuxedo as a Casual then removing the specs and changing into a shiny, gold dinner jacket for Garry. Usually no one figured it out. While all this fun was happening, I was beginning to work more and more on songwriting and working toward a goal of getting off the road and into the studio.

Hello, Elvis

Chester Power, Richard Williams, Elvis, and Buzz
at WHBQ Radio Studios, 1957

One night in Memphis, I had the time of my life,
Young Elvis Presley sure treated me and the boys alright.

"One Night in Memphis"
by Buzz Cason

In the '50s and '60s, to promote a new record release, usually a 45-rpm disc, an act would visit radio stations to meet the disc jockeys, who were stars in their own right and in some cases had their own local television show or record hops. What a concept! Jamming members of a band into an old car and driving all over the country with hopes of hearing that magical sound: your song on the air!

Even if you were a "nobody" with your first record, as I was with The Casuals in '57, you could secure on-air interviews and meetings with music directors, a feat that became more difficult as rock music grew. It was on a promotional jaunt to Memphis that we not only found ourselves on radio and TV, but also had the opportunity to meet Elvis Presley.

I first heard an Elvis Presley record on a portable radio on the beach at Daytona with my friend and fellow art class student, Jim Seymore. My mother had driven us there in our trusty '50 Chevy for some fun in the sun. I believe it was the closest I ever came to one of those patented Coppertone tans! We met two girls from Dupont High, a school located on the outskirts of Nashville and later when I went to visit Judy, the one I "liked," her boyfriend, a rather large football player threatened to beat me up, so I in turn beat it. In those days, if you weren't a starter on the football team you basically went nowhere with the girls. That's why it was fortunate that rock 'n roll came along and improved the social life of those of us who picked up guitars and hung up the cleats.

Elvis Presley was the essence of what some were calling rockabilly. But in younger pop music circles, the coined phrase "rock 'n roll" (usually attributed to New York deejay Alan Freed) more aptly applied to Elvis's music. He was our cultural role model at the time. We also had James Dean, but he was the L.A. rebel, pouty and reclusive, and besides that he couldn't sing. Elvis had it all: the looks, the moves, the clothes, and naturally that voice! The only irritating thing about it was the fact that the girls screaming took away from the kick of us guys having someone we were fans of. Before I'd ever seen or heard Elvis, another classmate of mine, Bill Taylor and I had what we jokingly called "The World's Smallest Elvis Fan Club" at Isaac Litton High School, in the Inglewood section of Nashville. Bill had been telling me about seeing Elvis on The Jackie Gleason Show, but having no television at home I'd never seen the Memphis Cat perform. So when I heard him sing "That's Alright, Mama," that day on the beach I knew why Bill was excited: It was Elvis's unique combination of rhythm and blues and country that turned me on.

We tried to get his "look." Other singers tried to emulate his image and sound, but no one matched up to him. He was particularly appealing to Southerners because he was ours. The sultry, Mississippi-born rocker wasn't a parent-challenging rebel, but actually a mama's boy. Sure, he gyrated and shook when he sang, but that was all part of his show. And there was his dad, Vernon, in the picture too. He seemed to be enjoying his son's success. Elvis represented a young man's dreams: fame, lots of girls, motorcycles, a Cadillac, and oh yes, a new house for mama!

Richard Williams, my singing partner with The Casuals who also played keyboards, Chester Power, who played one of the only rock-'n-roll accordions I'd ever heard, and I drove the 230 miles down to Memphis from Nashville in the spring of '57, to promote "My Love Song for You," which by then had been released on Dot Records. The most popular deejays in many cities usually hosted television dance shows, which were mini-versions of Dick Clark's American Bandstand. The shows featured the local high school kids dancing the latest steps to the current hit records. Since it was the pre–music video era, the only entertainment other than the jockey introducing the records was an occasional recording act visiting the show to publicize its new record. We did two of these shows that Saturday in Memphis. One was for Wink Martindale, who is now the veteran game-show host, the other for a longtime buddy of Elvis, George Klein. Both guys were natives of the Bluff City and very popular deejays. Each of them gave us a warm and enthusiastic reception both on- and off-camera. Of course they didn't hesitate to drop Elvis's name. In turn, we didn't waste much time asking if it would be possible to meet Elvis while were in town that day.

"Aw, no problem," George answered over coffee after the show. "Here's what y'all do, just be down at the Hotel Chisca at nine tonight and you'll get to meet him." Elvis came down every night to visit Dewey Phillips, host of Red Hot and Blues, on WHBQ-AM, the hottest nighttime show on the air in that area. Phillips was well known for being the first radio personality to play Elvis record back in '54. Wink confirmed that this definitely would be the place for us to be on that particular night and added that Elvis usually has an early date and drops by the station afterwards to hang out with Dewey and the guys, who were in the early stages of forming The King's entourage, later to be sometimes referred to as the Memphis Mafia.

With the help of George and Wink, an interview with Phillips was set up, giving us a legitimate reason to be at the station. By now, promoting the record had become secondary to the possibility of meeting one of our all-time heroes and no doubt the most happening singer in the world at the time. By this time, we had met musicians and performers who had either met Elvis or had actually worked road shows with him during those early days of the rockabilly sound. It is interesting, that at this writing, a worldwide revival of that magic sound of music the Memphis boys created is going on. Jeff Daniels had told us about working with Elvis at the Loui-siana Hayride. It was his opinion that Bob Luman, another outstanding country rocker, was as good or better than Elvis. Jeff tried to copy Elvis's shaking style on stage. Tommy Williams, a fine lead guitar and fiddle player, had a rather humorous and up-close account of traveling with Elvis and the Blue Moon Boys. It seems that the future king of rock didn't always bathe regularly during those road weary one-night-stand days. He also might go a few days without changing clothes. Thus came the threatto fellow members of our band when they walked around a crowded motel room wearing dirty underwear: "Boy, you better change those 'E.P.' drawers!" When the first version of my story came out in 2004, the producer of a top early morning news show in New York suggested that I tell that particular story. "Of all the rockin' episodes in my book, why do I have to tell that one?" But she insisted , so I stumbled through it and the hosts got a laugh out of it.

So here we were, three poor boys from Nashville, in our pink suit coats and black slacks, proudly carrying our little valise, which contained several copies of our new Dot 45-rpm record and a stack of glossy eight-by-ten photos, hoping Dewey would play our song. Sitting in Chester's '55 Chevy in front of the Chisca on South Main Street we wondered out loud if we really would get to see Elvis or not. Looking across the street we saw a commotion as a group of teenagers gathered behind a baby blue Cadillac parked directly in front of the hotel. One of the kids was holding on to the rear bumper, attempting to rock the car when a young man dressed in all black jumped out of the driver's side."Look y'all, that's him!" shouted Richard. The angry driver ranthe kid off and sped away in his Caddy leaving us with our mouths hanging open."Well, we saw Elvis, boys," I assured my partners. Our deejay friends had been right. This was one way to see our idol, although we would have preferred actually meeting him.

We gathered up our stuff, which included a small flash camera we always used to document our pursuit of our showbiz dreams and all the events related to it. Fans were everywhere. We pushed our way through the crowd on the sidewalk and rushed on in to the hotel lobby. Someone from the radio station escorted us up to the mezzanine, where the broadcast booth was located. Teddy bears with fan letters attached were everywhere. Names, phone numbers, and personal messages for Elvis were written in lipstick and markers on all available walls around the door leading to the station. Obviously, the management of the hotel had given up on keeping order to the place and general chaos reigned. We had never seen anything quite like it. Scenes like these would only fuel my desire to be part of this new phenomenon as did the screaming of the fans back home in venues like the Donelson Theatre. I fed off the energy of the music and the reaction of our audiences. If I made a few bucks, that was OK too. I never envisioned making a living out of music in any shape or form. This night was special. To be interviewed by a reputable jock in a city other than our hometown was really something! We had heard that Dewey was a crazy man, still we weren't prepared for whom we were about to meet. Wild-eyed with sandy hair, in his mid-thirties, screaming loudly into the microphone, this "mouth of the South" didn't let us down. He wasted no time in getting us on the air. He rang a big cowbell in between songs and continually shouted that "Eh-vis" would be back any minute. We were ushered into the control room just as Dewey was shouting into the microphone: "C'mon, Eh-vis, let's go get a piece in the valley," a rather irreverent reference to Elvis's gospel EP recording, "Peace in the Valley," which had just been released on RCA.

We went through a frantic and brief interview with Dewey asking the usual deejay-type questions about us, our record, and the other members of our band. He constantly injected that "Eh-vis'll be back here soon! Y'all hang on!" Richard was grinning the whole time and Chester's face was glowing redder with excitement as the night went on. I thought, "Man, if he's telling all of Memphis about Elvis being at the station tonight, this place is really gonna be wild before this radio show is over!" We did get our record played on WHBQ, which had been our initial objective, but all this Elvis stuff was definitely a cool bonus and an added perk to our little promotional trip. Our song, a rhythm-and-blues–sounding ballad, seemed to fit quite well on the station's rather eclectic format. Dewey pretty much played what music he wanted.

After the interview, we literally walked out of the control room right into Elvis, who was strolling down the narrow corridor, coming in our direction. Someone introduced us, we shook hands, and it seemed that Elvis was comfortable talking to us, enough to tell us about his recent purchase of a new house in Whitehaven, later known as Graceland. He even invited us to go out the next day to the home, just south of Memphis and tell his Uncle Vester to let us go up to the house and look around. He continually joked around with his friends and kept repeating, "Best of luck on your new job!" to the guys. Luckily, we had a small camera with us and as we snapped a shot with him, Elvis kept mumbling the line to his constant hangers-on, many of whom stayed with him for years.

That night at WHBQ I was bold enough to request an autograph and Elvis humorously signed it with the same "Best of luck on your new job!" phrase. Dressed in all black and sporting jet-black–dyed hair from his just completed Loving You film, Elvis cut a striking figure in the eyes of three "barely professional" musicians from Nashville, who were definitely awed by such a rare event. For the Popsicle Boy from Inglewood, who had listened to all those early Sun Records artists on his little crystal radio, I felt that if I never got anywhere in music I could always tell my kids I had met Elvis and of course show them the photo! I recall Elvis's friends and future Memphis Mafia members—Marty Lacker, Red West, and Alan Fortress—being there that night. We would later on renew our friendships with these guys when we visited Elvis's home in Los Angeles. We spent the night at the Peabody Hotel and watched the famous ducks ride the elevator as they traditionally do every morning and night at that grand old southern establishment.

The following morning, we cruised out Highway 51 to Whitehaven, just south of Memphis, in Chester's '55 Chevy to get a close look at this mansion Elvis had told us about. Believe it or not, there were no fans at the gates. We had no problem getting past Uncle Vester, who told us to "go on up to the house and look around." We proceeded to clown around on the front porch, striking our best rock-'n-roll poses and snapping pictures with the little camera. We peeked in the not-yet-curtained windows and got a kick out of the pastel colored walls in the front rooms with shades of bright reds and purples that Elvis most certainly had picked out. After driving by Elvis's present home, at that time on Audubon Drive, to gawk at what were the Memphis Cat's first Cadillacs, we headed back to Nashville with an experience under our belts that only a selected group of teenagers could boast of. I later wrote a song, "One Night in Memphis," which recalled the excitement of that night.

It was May 11, 1999, and I was recording at Sun Studio located at 706 Union Street in the heart of the Bluff City, Memphis, Tennessee. Standing in approximately the same spot where Elvis and the other legends of Sam Phillips's famed record company had sung their first hit songs was truly a thrill for me. I had piggybacked on to a session previously booked by Fetzer Mills, a journalist and music historian who had always dreamed of making a rockabilly style record at Sun. We had met at the taping of a video production of Rock 'n Roll Graffiti, produced in Nashville by Larry Black. Fetzer wrote an article about the event, which featured thirty-three classic rock music performers singing their hits and chatting in the round about those exciting early days of rock 'n roll. Like me, they had not only lived "the dream," but had survived all the pitfalls of showbiz and were having a ball telling their stories. After the taping, I followed up with Fetzer and a trip to Memphis was planned.

The musicians playing on this landmark session with me were James Lott, lead guitar and engineer; Ray Sanders, upright bass; and J.M. Van Eaton, drums. J.M. had played on many of the Jerry Lee Lewis

Chester Power, Richard Williams, Dewey Phillips and Buzz at WHBQ radio studios, Memphis 1957

hits, including "Whole Lotta of Shakin' Goin' on," the Killer's first smash for Sun. It only took running through the simple four-chord song two times prior to the red light signaling "go" in the dingy but magical studio. Todd, who assisted in engineering the tracks, had a slight grin as we ripped into the first and only take of "One Night in Memphis." I "flogged" my old '70 model Yamaha acoustic, a guitar I had purchased at Gruhn Guitars in Nashville along with aspiring singer-songwriter Jimmy Buffett, who also became the proud owner of a similar "axe." That night at Sun we seemed to achieve the early '50s "slap back" sound that put Memphis music on the musical map. And for the former East Nashville Popsicle boy–turned–entertainer, the thrill of living the rock-'n-roll dream was once again alive and well!

An interesting side note to my Sun Studio experience is that somewhere along the way, the tape containing the cut on "One Night in Memphis" somehow got lost, or most likely recorded over. This used to happen in the early days of my career, but not lately, so it kind of added to the "old school" authenticity of the whole thing. I decided it

Chester and Richard posing on the front steps of Graceland, 1957

would be fitting and funny to put "Recorded, mixed and erased at Sun Recording Service, Memphis, TN." Later in the '70s, Elvis gave Bobby Russell and me a thrill when he recorded, "Do You Know Who I Am?" for RCA, written by Bobby and published by our Russell-Cason Music company. With his raw and innovative style, Elvis had broken new ground for vast generations of singers and writers of commercial music, whether it was pop, rock, or country. He did it by utilizing his heritage of gospel and blues, all of which evolved into a totally fresh and original new genre of music, forever changing the world of recording in the process.

100,000 Miles a Year in a Station Wagon, Rockin' All the Way

Bob Beckham gets a little fresh air on the way out West

Come on along for a party, we're gonna do it up right.
All we got's a little three piece band
But you know we're gonna rock it tonight.
"An American Saturday Night"
by Buzz and Mac Gayden

Here comes the midget and those hoodlums,!" Don Rickles barked out in his New York Borscht Belt comic accent. "I'm going to let Rickles burn Brenda and you guys tonight," Dub Allbritten, Brenda Lee's manager, had declared, much to our surprise, since she was rarely subjected to any controversy such as that which Rickles liked to create. It was 1960 and we had walked in to the main show lounge at the Sahara Hotel in Las Vegas. Brenda was the headliner in the main room at the hotel, one of the top places to play on the Strip. Dub was obligated to arrange press for us, and Rickles's salty and zany comments usually were quoted in the media. We had a big laugh that night and Rickles's added to the great time we were having in Vegas after several long, hard months of preparation for this engagement. We had rehearsed Brenda's new act at Columbus Circle Studios in New York City under the guidance of choreographer Richard Barstow, whose previous clients had included Judy Garland and the Ringling Brothers Circus. Now, he was attempting to teach six rockers how to play, sing, and do dance steps. It was frustrating for all of us as evident on opening night at Blinstrub's Club in Boston, where we broke the act in just prior to Vegas.

During the show, when Brenda performed solo with the house orchestra, I had one small assignment, that of placing a stool for her to sit on. We rushed off the stage, thrilled with how our first show was going. In the excitement, I managed to forget to place it center stage. Just as I saw Brenda, bathed in the glow of a pin spot, reaching in the dark behind her for the stool, I heard "Buzz!!! The stool!" It was the high-pitched, slightly whiny voice of our director, Barstow, from the wings on the opposite side of the stage. The audience never knew about the mistake, but I sure did. We continued to rehearse days and play shows at night and managed to have fun, thanks to members of the Blinstrub chorus line, who showed us around South Boston and its nightlife. In the front row audience at one of our first shows were Brenda's top rival at the time, Connie Francis, and American Bandstand's Dick Clark. What a show she put on that night! We were thrilled about the prospect of club dates and staying in one place longer than twenty-four hours. We had been paying some serious dues, working one-nighters, from coast to coast, wearing out our young bodies and our equipment. What an honor it was to work with the phenomenal Brenda Lee, who would later become the first female singer elected to both the Country Music and Rock and Roll Halls of Fame. As she had done on hundreds of one-night engagements, the tiny dynamo thrilled the Vegas audiences and press alike with her exceptional talent and we were blessed to be onboard for the ride.

I've never traveled on one of the luxurious tour buses the stars and their bands and crews ride and sleep on today, but I plan to take a well-deserved mini-tour or short hop on one some day to compare the mode of travel to those of the late '50s and early '60s. We called it "stacking bodies" when six guys would squeeze into a station wagon and head out on a trip, which would be anywhere from 200 to 500 miles a day. One of our first wagons was a blue-and-white '59 Plymouth wagon powered by a rather potent V8 engine, which hauled our band and the trailer fairly well. One unique thing about the vehicle was how we had decorated its ceiling with all kinds of photos of our female fans. If you were fortunate enough, you could resting in what was known as "the cage," the storage area in the rear of the wagon where you could lie on your back and gaze up at the lovely pictures of the hearts we had broken! In those days when commercial music was changing so rapidly, a handful of country artists were "crossing over" to the popular music charts. We backed up many of these singers. One such act was Webb Pierce, a Decca recording star, who had several number one songs to his credit. "I Ain't Never," written by Mel

Tillis, was moving up the Billboard Hot 100. "Thanks for that little rock-'n- roll intro, fellahs," he'd say in his high-pitched Georgia drawl as we brought him on stage. The tour was a grueling one through the West and up into Canada, and it was in the middle of winter. Also on the bill was George Jones, already making his mark in country, he had a novelty tune, "White Lightnin'" hitting the popular music charts, and he had seen a significant bump in sales of the record, due to rock stations playing it. I was singing tenor duets with George, and one night I was trying to corral him to rehearse, which was a joke. Suddenly he got in my face and declared, "Boy, I wanna go pop!" I always thought that was ironic coming from an icon of traditional country.

That night as we left Billings, Montana, the snow was beginning to fall and we decided to all travel in a motorcade of sorts, since we had a long jump to the next town and didn't have time to stay over. Our station wagon was following the car of George and another singer, Eddie Noack, whose current hit was "Here I Am I'm Drunk Again," and he did his best to live up to the drinking image in his song and with Webb and George he was certainly in good company, as far as the enjoyment of consuming whiskey went. By the time we reached the open plains of Montana, the snow was blowing horizontally across the road. One of the cars in our entourage had a flat, so we all came to a halt in the middle of nowhere in blizzard conditions. Through our windshield, I could barely make out a figure in bright purple. It was Eddie staggering about, still in his colorful show suit. I jumped out of the car to see if I could help and as I passed Eddie, he grabbed my arm and yelled loudly over the howling wind, "Man, I've been out of this car five minutes and no one has offered me a drink yet!"

We were booked on varied types of tours like that one because of our musical flexibility and showmanship. Many of these trips proved to be amusing and challenging ventures. One trip in particular was eventful, a near tragedy and a record breaker. We were playing in Tullahoma, Tennessee, at a mid-week dance, when we were visited by a member of Jerry Lee Lewis's booking agency. It seemed he wanted us to be in Phoenix by Friday night, allowing us two days to get there! We were to start a two-week tour there opening for Jerry Lee, who was nicknamed "The Killer" because he called everyone else that. We frantically placed a call to our manager to see if we could get out of a couple of dates conflicting with the unexpected bookings. He said he would work it out. We would have to drive home, pack, and hit the road that night! I don't believe these crazy things could happen today, but they sure did in the early days of rock 'n roll.

To add to the craziness of making this 2,100-mile trip to the Southwest was the announcement of the next jump. It was to Buffalo, New York! At least this time we would have a few more days to make it. It must have been one or two in the morning when we finally got that Plymouth loaded for the trip westward. I climbed behind the wheel and didn't need relief as a driver until 2,100 miles later. I had set the band record for longest stint at the wheel by one band member. Along the way, I drank at least a gallon of black coffee and stuck my head out the window to be refreshed by the cold winter air. In fact, the season almost did us in when we hit a snowstorm in between Fort Worth and Dallas and we slid off the road down an embankment. I somehow managed to keep the rig under control until a very helpful Texas Ranger and a truck-driving farmer managed to pull us out of the ditch. Unbelievably, two of the guys slept through the whole thing! As I recall, we played about three, maybe four dates, in Arizona and New Mexico, then it was off to the Northwest. Jerry Lee had "torn 'em up" at the Southwestern stops. In most towns or cities, the fact that he had recently married his thirteen-year-old cousin, Myra Smith, didn't seem to dampen the fans' rock-'n-roll spirit.

Our job was to play until Jerry Lee and his band arrived—which included his father-in-law, J.W. Smith, on bass; Roland Janes on guitar; and Russell P. Smith on drums. The problem was Jerry Lee loved to stop along the way to the gig and see a matinee at a local theater. At that time, he was especially fond of horror flicks. Most nights, we could hold the crowd until the wild Memphis bunch rolled in but, after an hour or so, the crowd would start chanting, "We want Jerry Lee!" and we'd start praying for their arrival. I had created a long, rambling tune I changed nightly called "Big Train," which we could stretch indefinitely until it ended in a frenzy. We would work in the name of the town we were in and crowds loved it. We were flattered when Jerry Lee would sometime add a few lines of the song to the end of "Whole Lotta of Shakin' Goin' on."

There were times, however, when he would forget where he was. He would always open his show with, "It's indeed a privilege and a pleasure to be here with you in…uh…," as one of the musicians would bark out, "Phoenix, Jerry," or wherever we might be. With all his craziness and surprises, there still has yet to be an entertainer quite like this man who was once billed on Sun records as "Jerry Lee Lewis and His Pumping Piano. " And pump it he did, so much so that I still have a clear picture in my mind of our manager, X. (Xavier) Cosse, with the top of his desk covered with bills for pianos and piano repair from various auditoriums we had played.

"That damn Jerry Lee is gonna kill me!" X. would say as he winced and reached for a large bottle of Maalox that had been buried under the bills. Jerry would autograph keys and hammers from pianos he had destroyed. Yet with the Killer, there was a rock-'n-roll paradox of sorts, in that many nights after a wild concert, when the fans had left and we were packing up around him, Jerry would change into street clothes and return to the stage and what was left of the piano to do a more laid-back gospel-filled concert for those of us packing up. These are the priceless moments of life on the road, when knowing you have a grueling schedule ahead, you take a little time to pause and take in the music as it flows from the heart and soul of a gifted performer. Jamming and "sitting in" with each other lifts the spirits of all of us who sing and play music.

The Killer - recording at Sun, 1958

Jerry Lee would continue to be the source of numerous bizarre rock-'n-roll stories, like the one related by Billy Smith about a "gunpoint performance." The story goes: Jerry was booked in Evansville, Indiana, for a Sunday afternoon performance for a promoter named Norm Kiley. That particular time of the week was always slow in those days, but on this date, only a handful of fans had shown up, made up mainly of members of Kiley's family. "Cat, why don't you just give the folks back their money and I'll just go on down the road." Kiley opened his briefcase and pulled out a .45-caliber pistol and reminded the Killer that the show would go on. Jerry Lee complied.

The next challenge of this short but mega-mileage jaunt was the drive across the entire country to upstate New York. As was the case of many of these long jumps, the only thing that kept us anywhere sane was the occasional stops to eat and consume more coffee. Many times we ate breakfast twice, once at a friendly-looking truck stop in the middle of the night and again at a city cafe or another truckers' choice later on in the morning. As I recall, the fateful Phoenix-Buffalo jump was our longest to date, probably close to 3,000 miles with no stopping for rest. When Robert Oermann interviewed me for Brenda Lee's biography, he couldn't believe the primitive way we traveled and kept asking how we did it all ourselves: driving, loading, stage setup, hotel arrangements, and other duties. We had to do it all. It was a matter of not having the money to pay help and having no room for them to ride. It was the world of six men in a station wagon, packed in like sardines. On this trip were myself, Richard, Billy, Tony Moon, Joe Watkins (our saxophone player), and our bassist at the time, Perry Potts.

We were making good time, probably over twenty-four hours into our trip when disaster struck. We were somewhere in Illinois, not to far from the Ohio border when we drove into a wall of smoke. Richard hit the brakes to slow down in order to see, since the visibility was down to near nothing. No sooner than we had reduced our speed to about ten miles per hour, the crash came. Simultaneously with the hard jolt that sent a pain into my right arm that I had propped against the open passenger window frame, was a loud scream from the rear of the Plymouth wagon. It was brought on by the pain of Perry Potts, who had been sleeping on the third seat and had been awakened by the painful crushing of his hip by the bumper that had been catapulted by our trailer hitch into the rear door, pinning Perry in, excruciating pain and all. We had been rear-ended by a lady from that area, who unlike us, had not slowed down and obviously hadn't seen our car. We were fortunate in one way, since it appeared only Perry was injured. He was in a great deal of pain, but he assured us he would survive. So we left him in the hospital, rented a beat up old Nash sedan and continued on our way to Buffalo in the true "the show must go on" mode. The Nash broke down in Pennsylvania, we left it with a mechanic, rented another car and kept going.

Perry was not only a great bass player, but he was my "horse." Many nights during a spirited performance, I rode his shoulders, and much to the crowd's delight he would flip me off onto the stage, where I'd do a little fake splits or whatever move came to mind. And by the way, Richard could do the real splits, as taught to him by none other than Little Anthony of the Imperials. The September 5, 1958 Asheville Citizen (North Carolina) printed a review of the Jerry Lee Lewis show that read:

From 3 p.m. until his arrival, The Casual Teens entertained with Buzz Cason as vocalist. This band—with Richard Williams as pianist, Johnny McKay and Perry Potts, guitars, Joe Watkins at tenor sax, and Bill Smith at the drums—plays the standard rock-and-roll fare very well indeed, and has some extraordinary comedy acts. In one, everybody but the drummer played from prone positions on the floor, the microphone on top of the singer. In another, the vocalist sang from the shoulders of the guitarist, getting up and down without either of them missing a note. The audience responded with screams and squeals and rapped out the beat with clapping hands and snapping fingers, showing their favoritism with the most noise for "Rock It Up," "Hard Headed Woman," and "One More Time."

This article accurately reflected the energy and humor of the early days of rock music. "What kept you?" Dub Allbritten jokingly asked when we arrived in Buffalo just a couple of hours prior to the show that night. Several music trade papers ran the story. Once again we had survived, but the trials of that trip were not over.

We had unpaid bills in the town of McComb, Illinois, for the Nash we had picked up on the return trip, and we stupidly, against Billy Smith's wishes, went back through McComb, knowing they were looking for us. A local police officer recognized the Nash, and pulled us over and promptly arrested our fearless leader, Billy Smith, who had signed for the car. Jerry King, our old friend and manager who by then was on the Nashville police force, came to our rescue by assisting in Billy's bail and helping to arrange to pay for the car. Things seldom went real smooth, and we began to refer to our misfortunes as that "Casual Luck." But it never held us back from charging on and always making our shows and giving the crowds their money's worth.

To me, this was more than pursuing some kind of stardom, it was hard work, the American way, but for us, at that stage of our lives, we were meeting and learning from folks from all walks of life and having our share of fun as we traveled all over the country. We did manage to hit all fifty states and play shows in most of them. From Perry Potts's cry of "Just get me out of here!" to the whiny orders of a choreographer, we had seen and heard a lot building up to that rather prestigious Vegas appearance. Add to the mix: fights with drunks and dealing with irate club owners, we had paid some serious dues. On the Sahara opening night, we became what Barstow had ordered us to be: the setting for the diamond, the framework for our star, Brenda, to shine from. We had created a Broadway presentation with a solid rock and pop foundation. The reviews were glowing, she was a success and The Casuals had come a long way from that first show in Lebanon, Tennessee. One of our touring highlights came when we were booked on The 1960 Show of Stars, produced by Irwin Feld and starring Brenda and the "Fabulous Fabian." It was one of many package shows traveling the country in the '50s and '60s. Also on the bill were Duane Eddy, The Bill Black Combo, Jimmy Clanton, Chubby Checker, Freddy Cannon, Jimmy Charles, Bob Beckham, Bobby Vinton's orchestra and a comedian named Herkie Styles. Our road manager was the black kid who played "Buckwheat" in Our Gang, Harold Cromer. Our stage manager was Charlie Carpenter, who literally had to push me out onto the stage in Minneapolis, as I was about to make my debut as Garry Miles in front of a large packed house for the first time.

The large black man put a gentle hand on my shoulder, and discovering my shaky condition gave me a good shove into the spotlight, shouting "Go on out and do it to 'em, Garry!"

My mouth went dry as I attempted, "Let's Go, Let's Go, Let's Go," a Hank Ballard R&B tune, followed by my current hit, "Look For A Star," which was high in the charts and playing on most of the Top 40 stations in the U.S. I was still a nervous wreck on "Star," but the girls' screams and recognition of my one and only hit calmed me and the band and I went over well in our big two-song set. Frank Sinatra supposedly said, "You gotta be a little on edge to do a good show." My mouth still goes dry when I perform in public.

Most of the acts on the Show of Stars had received a most helpful boost from television's Dick Clark by appearing on American Bandstand or The Dick Clark Show on Saturday nights. In the early days in particular, the artists were asked to endorse their paychecks from their appearance back to Clark's production company. This was no secret in our business, but on the humorous side, there were those singers who refused to give the money back.

Among them was high energy rockabilly, Sun recording artist Billy Lee Riley, who confirmed this action in a phone call to his home in Arkansas many years later. I asked him, "Did you ever appear on the show again?"

"Nope," he laughingly replied. Then we both agreed most of us would have paid to be on one of those shows in the early days of our career for the national exposure it obviously provided.

That tour of thirty or so dates all across the Midwest and the Southeast was definitely a highlight of our road days. Except for Brenda and Fabian, most of the artists performed only two or three of their current hits. Duane's twang guitar instrumentals were really hot then, so he performed a few more songs, as did Brenda. As for Fabian, he only had a couple of hits including "Like a Tiger" and "I'm a Man," which he did for screaming fans, and as always, in the key of B-flat, a tone he had memorized so he could sing somewhere within pitch of the key, battling the always voluminous roar of the crowd. Our

band had discovered this phenomenon while backing Fabe in Birmingham and Montgomery. I buddied up with Larry Knechtel, the bass player for Duane, and we rode many hours on the bus singing R&B songs while he played a keyboard that he blew into like a wind instrument. Larry would later become part of David Gates's pop band, Bread, as a keyboard player. He also played the guitar solo on the group's "Guitar Man."

The bus we traveled on was not like one of today's luxury tour buses the stars travel in, but more of the ordinary Greyhound Charter variety. It had no bathroom facilities, so several times during a long jump, those who always rode up front near the driver would shout out "Pittsburgh," at which time a weary group of young rockers would slowly stumble off the bus and relieve themselves along the side of the road, many times late at night in all kinds of weather.

Many of the funny things that happen on tours such as these fall into the "you'd have to have been there to appreciate it" category, but some events are worth mentioning, such as the Fabian newspaper interview episode. It seems when we arrived in the real Pittsburgh, there was a young lady who had been granted an interview with the teen idol for her high school newspaper. The setting was a real nice suite in the elegant hotel Fabian was staying in. Several of Fabian's band members and singers were there, but his drummer was missing from the room. Niceties were exchanged and the young lady proceeded to conduct the interview, which she obviously had looked forward to doing. Just when things reached a quiet point, one of the large doors opened at the end of the suite and the drummer, Charlie Pasquo, charged through the middle of the room, holding a drumstick out in front of him in a sword-like fashion, stark naked! Shrieks came forth from both the interviewer as well as the shocked one being interviewed. Then came gut-busting laughter from the

other band members as Charlie, never breaking stride, went out the other door on the opposite end of the room. The original Streak no doubt!

At almost every show, Bobby Vinton would ask Charlie Carpenter if he could sing and every night it was usually the same answer: "Not tonight, Bobby." He rarely got to sing and always seemed dissatisfied

just conducting and playing saxophone in the band. We would chat backstage and I thought it was funny when he asked me to help him with some stage dance moves for his solo act. I always found it amusing that in a year or so Bobby would be headlining some of those same shows after having his huge hit, "Roses Are Red."

Many nights a search group would go out searching for Bobby's dad, who also played in the orchestra, but loved to hit the bars pretty hard after the shows. His drinking habits sometimes caused him to be either still lost in the morning when we were leaving or just late for the bus. "Is Mr. Vinton on the bus?" the call would go out from one of the road managers. If he was present it was likely that we were all on the bus and could leave.

As I had sensed in playing the Brooklyn Paramount, we now seemed to be playing the very last days of the Vaudeville format, in that those appearances were actually variety shows, consisting of several, diverse acts popping on and off the stage in a rapid, nonstop fashion. The energy and pure rock-'n-roll excitement of a show like that was truly unforgettable and a fun experience for those of us onstage as well as the audience. To play thirty-seven days straight without a break is a feat in itself. Performers today don't realize what a luxurious life they have on the road compared to what we experienced. In addition to not knowing any better, our aspirations weren't as high as some kids today, the record companies weren't putting any money behind many of us. In general most of us thought the whole "rock star" bit was a fly-by-night thing and most likely not a permanent career.

By the end of the tour the luggage racks were filled with empty whisky bottles that rolled around as the bus rocked and rolled into our last show dates, which were in Virginia. In Norfolk, the whispering began that there on the next to the last night of one of rock's greatest shows, as it was billed, it would be open season on wrecking each other's acts with unmerciful and humiliating pranks! To begin with, Dub declared that Brenda was to be absolutely off-limits to the pranksters, but all of us other acts were sitting ducks. Duane's band pulled a fairly mild trick on me, when they picked up horns from the orchestra that they weren't familiar with and proceeded to play a horrible solo during "Look For A Star." All of us Casuals were laughing our tails off as the stunned audience wondered what was going on. Little did they know what was in store for the remainder of the evening.

Freddy "Boom Boom" Cannon always exited the stage with a little Philly-style dance shuffle and screamed the last of one his patented, rather obnoxious "whoos" to the screaming fans. At the exact moment of this final shout he was hit with a bucket of water by members of the Bill Black Combo with the spotlight catching his every gurgle and gasp! Ace Cannon was the sax player in Black's band and pulled the best stunt of the night. After locking Fabian's vocal backing group, the Fabulous Four, in a dressing room along with the star himself, Ace prepared for the grand finale. We had all previously harassed the four singers from Philly when we secretly advised the waitress in one of the many truck stops in the South where we would eat breakfast to put our servings of grits, which they had never seen and had learned to hate, onto their plates. This time they could only scream and beat on the locked door as Ace prepared to appear as Fabian himself. On a normal show, the Fabulous Four sang a rousing intro building up to a hair-raising crescendo, but on this special night, the replacement quartet, made up of members of Duane's band, sang an out-of-tune "Fabian…Fabian…Fabian…" and the crowd screamed louder, drowning out the introduction. The moment the bright white spotlight hit the curtain on stage right, Ace Cannon waddled out into the light with a rose in his mouth wearing a white tee shirt with a huge "F" painted on it with bright red lipstick. The screaming came to an abrupt halt as the fans saw the funny, sort of bug-eyed man with the beer belly playing the part of their teenage dream boy! Fabian eventually was released from his captivity and the show went on.

It was a particularly memorable night for me: in addition to being a victim of a prank, one of the show's managers and Jimmy Clanton's road manager, wanting to get in on the fun, had refused to let me in the show that evening, telling the security guards there that I was an imposter and to throw me out which they immediately did, leaving me to go to another entrance where I managed to talk my way in. My brother-in-law was with me and he was really confused until he discovered what was going on, then like all of the cast and crew he too got a kick out of the antics.

As rock 'n roll became more popular, the pranks increased and it seems that trashing hotel rooms has been a rock-'n-roll tradition for many years. I'm convinced it all began with a handful of country-rockabilly guys who were a little bored and possibly a little wired on amphetamines. We heard numerous stories, including one about George Jones and his associates repainting hotel rooms for entertainment. One of the most novel hotel escapades, however, was credited to none other than Johnny Cash and his band, who were renowned for not only outstanding music and popularity all across the U.S., but for their antics offstage as well.

It seems Johnny and the boys purchased several dozen baby chicks, smuggled them upstairs, then filled an elevator with them, and sent them down to the lobby, much to the surprise of those on the ground floor when the door opened. Another version of that story has the elevator being filled with furniture and an exploding series of the most powerful firecrackers the pranksters could find! So to my journalist friends who always delight in stories about the later rock-'n-roll days of hotel-room bashing, drugs, and sex, I assure you we had our fun too, but in slightly more sensible and safer ways. Although we weren't exactly your typical boys next door, we came from good families and usually knew where to draw the line on recreation.

While enjoying my short stint as Garry Miles in 1960, our string of one-nighters took us to both of our nation's newest states, Hawaii and Alaska. Downtown Fairbanks was one long, snow-covered, frigid main street with churches on one side and bars on the other. (I guess that means they had more religious drinkers than any place on the globe at the time!) We had a wild time after our show at a blues club, where we jammed and partied with the locals and a few of the deejays from the rock radio station. After that, Bob Beckham and I wound up at the home of one of the deejays girlfriends, where the fun went on into the wee hours. The deejay was doing the all night show, and at one point during his broadcast, he mused on air, "I wonder what Bob Beckham and Garry Miles are up to right now?" We all rolled with laughter, but the laughs came to a screeching halt when the same guy paid a surprise visit to his girlfriend's house. Luckily, she recognized

Fabian and The Casuals, Birmingham, Alabama, 1959

his car pulling up, prompting Bob and me to scamper out the back door into the subzero weather.

My last words as I leaped out into the snow were, "Get rid of him quick!" After we had huddled in the snow for a few minutes, I whispered to Bob, "This is it…this is where we die man, what a way to go!" After the deejay finally left, it took us several hours to thaw out and see the humor in the incident.

Brenda and her entourage had arrived in Anchorage aboard a United Constellation prop-driven airliner from Seattle. It was one of the only times we flew to a show. We had been greeted by the new state's governor and someone arranged a dogsled ride for all of us for a little publicity. It was really an exciting trip and I particularly got a kick out of flying around the state in the vintage World War II Navy PBY seaplanes that at times struggled to take off in the choppy waters. Brenda's mother, Grace Tarpley, was on the tour and she wasn't as thrilled as we were to be flying in the old planes, especially when the pilot had to abort a takeoff and splash back down into a lake one morning to avoid heading straight into a glacier! Joe Watkins and I loved to strap ourselves in the gun turrets and pretend to be in combat as we flew over the beautiful new state on the noisy, often bouncy aircraft. The same year, 1960, we toured Hawaii, like Alaska also a brand new state. Upon our arrival there, I was in for a pleasant surprise when I discovered that "Look For A Star" was number one on KPOI Radio, the top rock station in the islands. When we deplaned in Honolulu we were greeted by Tom Moffitt, a deejay with KPOI who had booked the tour there that included, in addition to Brenda, Chubby Checker, who was still hot with "The Twist."

We were thrilled to be in such a beautiful place playing shows, finding it hard to believe that our music had allowed us to perform in paradise. And what a gorgeous and still undeveloped world of beauty those islands were back then. From the time we were greeted by fans at the airport up until the last aloha, we were literally covered with sweet smelling, colorful leis, and our hotel rooms smelled like flower shops. The island of Maui unbelievably had no high-rise buildings, in fact no condominiums at all. We stayed in thatched huts on the Garden Island.

Dub Allbritten, Buzz, and Brenda, arriving in Hawaii, 1960

Chubby Checker and Buzz as Garry Miles, Hawaii 1960

The Casuals and The Big Boppers onstage in Daytona Beach, 1958

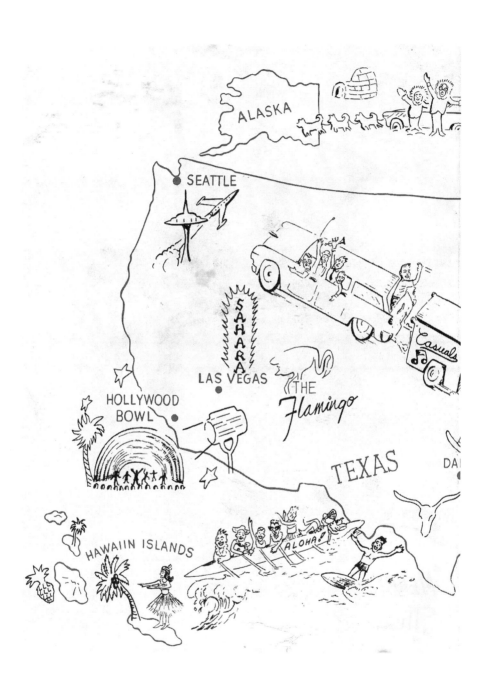

We played in a schoolhouse with no air conditioning and the windows open letting in the hot, humid air, as we wailed away. My song was well received and it turned out to be one of the more fun touring adventures for six wide-eyed Southern rockers playing our hearts out in such an exotic setting. We played near Pearl Harbor at Scofield Barracks, where the audience was quiet and the faces in the crowd made up of the military seemed to reflect depression from obviously missing the Mainland. Little did any of us realize how different the islands of this tropical paradise would become over the years. (When I returned for a few days in 1980, I couldn't believe the change.) I did spot one landmark, the hotel where *Gidget Goes Hawaiian* was being filmed. We had been invited to visit the set, which was at the Royal Hawaiian Hotel, where we met and chatted with James Darin, Deborah Walley, and other members of the cast.

Soon we were back to reality, touring all over again, back in the station wagon, pulling the trailer filled with the tools of our trade. In Fredonia, Kansas, we encountered for the first time a chicken-wire screen in front of the stage to catch the bottles. At what had to be a low point of his career, future producer and record company executive Jimmy Bowen appeared with us in this dive, with a lovely blonde on his arm, wearing a worn-out blue suit and singing his lone hit, "I'm Stickin' with You." The shows we were booked on enabled us to meet a continuous stream of talented folks. The Burnette brothers and Johnny, Memphis natives then living in L.A. were among our favorites to back up. Dorsey sang his big ones, "Tall Oak Tree" and "Hey Little One," and Johnny rocked it up with "You're Sixteen" and "Dreamin'," two of his monster hits. We had great times on and off the stage, sometimes using the old trick we used on the Jerry Lee tours. We assured the audience that the management of whichever hotel or motel we were staying would not appreciate us giving out the location of our accommodations for the night, so we would tell the audience not to show up there, giving out the address in the process. This would assure us of a huge turnout for the party we would usually have after the show. We did shows with Fats Domino, Wilson Pickett, Donnie Brooks, Carl Mann, Bobby Lee Trammell, Roy Orbison, and countless other great acts. All with different styles, all with stories to share. The essence of life in rock 'n roll was meeting and hearing these people we had heard over and over on the radio. Each act brought its unique sound to the stage and continually thrilled the audiences.

It was on a lonely stretch of Texas highway in 1959 where we heard the sad news about the tragic crash that took the lives of Buddy Holly, Richie Valens, and The Big Bopper.

We had only a few weeks backing up J.P. Richardson, also known as The Big Bopper and had loved him and his music. There was a record by Tommy Dee called "Three Stars", which was a tribute of sorts to the three singers. Every time it would play, we would shortly thereafter have a near collision on the highway. None of us were normally superstitious, but after a few near misses, we reached for the radio dial to change stations as quickly as possible, realizing how blessed we were to be alive and heading to the next gig, watching the odometer rolling on up to 100,000 miles every year!

Sammy, Ricky, and Elvis Again

On the way to Eureka, California, from San Francisco,
November 27, 1960

We didn't see the bridge or visit Chinatown
When we hit San Francisco all we did was fool around.

"Tiger A GoGo"
by Buzz Cason and Bucky Wilkin

I turned twenty-one in Eureka, California. It was a wild night in this small town on the Pacific Ocean in the Northern Redlands. Along with Brenda Lee, Dorsey Burnette, and Bob Beckham, The Casuals played a one-night stand at Black Jack Wayne's, a rough and rowdy nightclub. The owner, Black Jack, himself emceed the show and fired very realistic-sounding blank .45-caliber pistols into the ceiling to get the crowd stirred up. It was a fitting way to celebrate such a milestone of a birthday in that we played to a loud and boisterous group of patrons who seems to have been starved for a good show. As I previously noted, with Brenda, the audience was always assured of a powerful performance. Her voice, style, and overall showmanship were unparalleled qualities among all the entertainers of that era. That night in 1960 was no exception. We were all road weary from a grueling trip across Canada by car, winding up in Vancouver and traveling from there down the West Coast. We were looking forward to La-La Land—that is, Hollywood—with all its excitement and the much-needed Southern California sun. It was on this same trip our beloved "Elizabeth" (named after Elizabeth Taylor), a black '56 Caddy four-door hardtop, burned up in Eugene, Oregon. The fire was started by overheated brakes and was threatening to burn our show clothing, which was packed in the trunk. Bobby Watts, our bass player at the time, was our "hero" in that he rescued our duds from the red-hot trunk, receiving burned hands in the process. Meanwhile, the remaining five of us brave musicians were standing back from the Caddy expecting her to blow up at any second. We had lost our all-time favorite band car in the Great Northwest. As always, "the show must go on" was our motto, so we continued on in our rental car. It was rather a breezy ride leaving Black Jack's that night since vandals had broken our rear window.

Several years later I used the name "Black Jack Wayne" as the villain in the bedtime stories I told my sons, Taylor and Parker. The stories contained the imaginative characters Cody and Jody, who were always heroes and solved various crimes and did good deeds wherever they could, always winning out over Black Jack and his plot to defeat the good guys.

Dorsey Burnette, a former heavyweight boxer who had sparred with Sonny Liston during his brief fighting career, was riding with us that night. We had stopped in Seattle to record a few songs with Dorsey at the same studio where Bob Reisdorf had produced hits on The Ventures and The Fleetwoods for Dolton Records, later to be a subsidiary of Liberty Records, the label I was recording for as Garry Miles. As we made music all night in the studio that overlooked the lights of Seattle below, I once again longed for the day when I might have a similar setup in the form of my own facility to record in. The road was fun, but I was tired of it and wanted to be back home writing and producing. Instead, here I was speeding through the cool northern California night with two slightly drunk boys from Memphis who constantly picked at each other, providing a majority of our post-show entertainment nightly. The other character, Lamar Fike of Memphis Mafia fame, a moniker given to sidekicks of Elvis, was our interim road manager and sometime bodyguard for Brenda. When he and Elvis, with whom he had attended Hume High School in Memphis would have a disagreement resulting in Elvis firing him, Lamar contacted Dub Allbritten, Brenda's legendary manager, and get his job back on the road with us. In his three-piece black mohair suit, the 300-plus-pound Lamar swaggered through crowds snapping his fingers shouting, "OK, here she comes, clear the way for the little lady!" It was funny, but a pretty cool sight to see this huge, flashy guy heading for the backstage area with the tiny Brenda laughing most of the way to, as always, a fantastic performance.

As we approached San Francisco, the conversation shifted to an argument between Dorsey and Lamar as to just exactly how many stars Lamar actually knew. As the jabbing and shouting increased, my singing partner, Richard Williams, muttered "Oh no, this is gonna get wild." At this point, Dorsey bet Lamar $300 he could not introduce us to three stars in three days and proceeded to give him a list of celebrities who might qualify for this unique competition. Keep in mind I loved the Burnette brothers as much as any rockers we had traveled with, but they could not hold their liquor, which in this case was beer and/or Canadian blended whisky. I'll share more on Johnny later. "You don't know all these people you claim to know," Dorsey repeated over and over to Lamar. "OK, Mr. Smartass, I'll show ya!" Lamar shot back. "We'll go meet Sammy right now!" "Sammy who?" Dorsey questioned sarcastically. "You know who I'm talking about...Sammy Davis, Jr. I know where he's staying and we'll just head right up there and see him," Lamar retorted. It was time for Richard and me to intervene. "Hey, let's just go check in to the motel guys. It's after midnight. We don't need to meet Sammy or anyone tonight," I pleaded with them. "Yeah, this is nuts," Richard agreed.

But, the two feuding Memphis boys refused to listen. "Aw naw," Dorsey said, with a laugh, "we're going to meet Sammy." Sammy Davis, Jr. was a star if there ever was one. As a film star, a recording artist, a phenomenal live performer, he had it all. Add in the fact he was a member of Sinatra's Rat Pack, and it would indeed be a thrill to meet him if actually came about in this bizarre way.

The doorman at the Mark Hopkins Hotel must have wondered what kind of a motley crew he had let into his well-known and elegant establishment. In we strolled in our wrinkled rock-'n-roll show clothes, moving comically across the lobby, where Lamar somehow convinced the hotel operator to ring Sammy's room.

Dorsey was snarling and getting angrier by the minute as Lamar nodded and told an apparent Sammy, "Thanks, man, we'll be right up." Dorsey was incensed. It appeared he was on the way to losing the bet. It was a Hollywood scene. A full party was going on in a plush and spacious suite like we had never imagined, much less seen. Sammy met us at the door and introduced us to a few of his friends including a "foxy babe" with a diamond in her back, just like a good blues song. A wide screen was set up for viewing films, most likely one of Sammy's favorite Westerns. Sammy was a most gracious host and impressive man, especially to four rockers who has basically crashed his party. He even took a few minutes to hear about our dreams of opening up a teen nightclub in Hollywood where we were temporarily based. Dorsey still hadn't uttered a word. As we left and thanked Sammy for a good time, Dorsey said, "Yeah, thanks for the drinks!"

Sammy chuckled and said politely, "Well, maybe if I come see you in Memphis, you'll offer me one."

Dorsey snapped back, "We don't drink in our home, we're Catholic!" I wanted to fall through the floor of that penthouse. After an expected silence we made a quick exit, cussing Dorsey as soon as the door closed behind us.

Lamar won the bet because during next two nights, we went to parties at Ricky Nelson's and Elvis's homes. Chalk up another unusual and fun night traveling down the rock-'n-roll highway. We were staying in a cheap hotel on Sunset Boulevard in the heart of Hollywood or as J.I. Allison of The Crickets used to refer to it as "Hollyweird." There is a bend in that glittering street of dreams where the hotel was located and at the time was the beginning of the famed Sunset Strip, where just a few blocks away the rock-'n-roll venue Whiskey A-Go-Go would soon open. The first day we arrived in the L.A. area, Richard and I were cruising the Strip on a beautiful pre-smog day in a new Chevy convertible Lamar had allegedly rented from a rental company on Sunset. It was truly one of those star happenings for us. How much better could it get? Two handsome young guys riding down Sunset with our cheap shades on in a slick new ragtop ride with the radio blasting the cool sounds of the hot Top 40 station, which was most likely KFWB. Who would know we had no more than ten dollars between us? We had just flashed our big Southern smiles at two attractive ladies who were walking on the sidewalk on our right almost in front of the well-known 77 Sunset Strip address when we heard shouts from the opposite side of the street:

"Hey you!" the man screamed, "Tell Lamar to bring that car back right now!" Our bubble was burst. We nodded and scooted down in the seat hoping the two lovelies wouldn't see us in our humiliation. Lamar had pulled off a typical slick-talker trick: He had talked the car salesmen into a test drive that turned into a two-day joyride.

With the idea of assuring himself of winning the ongoing bet with Dorsey, Lamar arranged for our second celebrity party crashing for that evening. It seems Ricky Nelson was having a party at his home in the Hollywood Hills, in a neat area where many young film and recording stars of that day lived. "Rick," as he preferred to be called, was still involved in the daily filming of the Nelson family television show, Ozzie and Harriet, the long-running series featuring his mom, dad, and older brother, David. Rick had begun singing on the show and soon was signed to Lou Chudd's Imperial Records in Hollywood and instantly became a rock-'n-roll teen idol, with hits like "Hello Mary Lou," "Believe What You Say," and "Lonesome Town," songs written by many of the bright young songwriters of the early '60s. There was a party somewhere every night in the Hills, and even though many of the stars and starlets in attendance had early morning calls at various studios, the activities went on into the late-night and early-morning hours. Such was the case at the packed bachelor pad of Rick Nelson that night in '60. Many familiar faces were there including Wally, the "kid next door" from the Nelsons' television show. Rick was a gracious host. These were basically the pre-recreational drug days and the scene was not near as wild as one might expect, but a good time was had by all.

With two-thirds of the bet won, it was time for the finale. Lamar had asked Elvis if we could join the nightly party on Perugia Way in Bel Air. Elvis remembered meeting us at WHBQ in Memphis and invited us to come over. Needless to say, we accepted. We left our humble Hollywood digs for the glamorous section of West Los Angeles, where the rich and famous dwelled. The home Elvis rented when he was shooting a movie had at times served as a Western White House. Richard Nixon and Nikita Khrushchev had stayed there. But tonight, six musicians from East Nashville and an electrician-turned–pop music crooner from Oklahoma would be invading the private world of one of the biggest stars in history and we were pumped! The crooner was Bob Beckham who was also managed by Dub Allbritten. Like Brenda, Bob also recorded for Decca and had recently had a hit on a ballad, "Just as Much as Ever." He was frequently on tour with us as part of Brenda's road show. Like us, he was equally excited and nervous about being in Elvis's home.

The crew—which included Alan Fortress, Charlie Hodge, and Red West—greeted us at the door and showed us the spacious and beautifully decorated place, which had a large den with a bar, piano, and guitars waiting to be played, and a television room with the first large-screen color television we had seen in a home. One of the more fascinating rooms was the guest bedroom with two-way mirrors, where the highly mischievous Memphis Mafia clowns could eavesdrop on visitors who might slip away there for a little romantic action. These combination bodyguards-hangers-on good ol' Southern boys were constantly coming in and out of the various rooms, making phone calls and promptly responding to any need The King might have. Food and drinks were abundant and since we were usually broke, we took advantage of the situation. Elvis was not known to be a drinker, but I did notice him requesting "one of those special iced teas" from time to time as the night went on. Girls were in abundance and they were attractive, and naturally all their eyes were on Elvis.

Not long after we arrived, Lamar proceeded to organize what would be the "main event" of the evening, and little did Richard and I know, but we were called upon to perform for our host. "Elvis, these boys have a record in the charts," Lamar announced referring to "Blue Velvet," which we had recorded under the name of The Statues for Liberty Records. "Y'all sing it for Elvis," the big man demanded. One can imagine our horror. Here was a man who had sold millions of records and was one of the greatest performers and singers of our time and we were being asked to sing for him our song thatwas hovering near the bottom of the charts. Richard and I looked at each other's red faces and, realizing we did in fact owe our "party tour director," we moved toward the piano. We made it through the classic standard with its rhythm-and-blues arrangement we had copied directly from one of my favorite vocal groups, The Clovers.

Elvis smiled and politely approved of our performance. Realizing our love for R&B and particularly group harmony, Elvis, sliding on to the piano bench, looked me in the eye and asked, "Did'ya ever think about how many songs go like this?" He proceeded to play a C-A minor-F-G progression in a triplet slow-dance groove and broke into "Sincerely," "Blue Moon," "Good Night My Love," and several other easy rockers, and we promptly joined in with vocal parts. Two things seemed to be evident: he was glad to see some fresh faces from "back home" and he was ready to jam. The tempo picked up, and just like on a Saturday night at a rockin' country show in Louisiana, we wound up with a rousing gospel number taking all of us back to the South one more time. It was spiritual. We were filled with the joy of singing, leaving the hassles and hardships of the road life behind for a few minutes. A surreal exerience, no doubt. And for Elvis, to be playing and singing in a no pressure and fun way had to be a refreshing contrast to what he faced at 6 a.m. the next morning working on a film with another dumb script, encountering the usual dose of Hollywood phonies, and quite possibly missing the thrill of live performing. I asked Lamar how Elvis did it—this partying nearly every night, making an early morning call at the studio to get made up, and being on the set on time with lines memorized. Memorization alone can be difficult in the entertainment world given all the stress and distractions. I wasn't surprised when Lamar answered, "A little somethin' to get down and a little something to get up." Obviously, he was referring to the pills that started a trend that sadly in only a few years would lead to Elvis's untimely death.

Another neat thing happened when Elvis went over his stereo and asked, "Y'all wanna hear where I'm getting my song ideas?" We all nodded as he put on a vinyl recording of Enrico Caruso's "Return to Sorrento"; then after only a few seconds, he lifted the needle, grinning, and said, "Now listen to this!" We were about to be the first listeners outside of RCA officials and a handful of Presley insiders to hear the next Elvis single recording, "Surrender," a follow-up to "It's Now or Never." What a rare treat! As we applauded, I noticed Bob Beckham had not moved from the easy chair he had plopped down into with drink in hand. He motioned me to come over to him and whispered, "Son, don't let me drink too much, I'd hate to get drunk at Elvis's house." As I recall, he did anyway, but I continued to stop by his chair assuring him by staying put, his woozy condition would probably go unnoticed. For us, free drinks were a rarity and tempting to starving pickers. As for alcohol, we were an unusual band in that we adhered to a "No drinking" rule on work days in those early years. This wasn't a work day!

The party soon took an unusual turn that led to our slightly early exit. Christina Crawford, the adopted daughter of Joan Crawford, paid Elvis a visit. The group was scattered, and I found myself in the TV room seated across a large coffee table from Elvis and Christina watching *Bonanza*, one of the few shows in color then. Elvis had been puffing on a cigar making small talk with me as Christina tickled him and kidded around, apparently seeking more direct attention. Suddenly, she slung the contents of her cocktail glass right into Elvis's face. We're talking close range here, folks. The cigar went "phhhtttt" and he jumped up. I leapt up in surprise.

He grabbed her by the hair. "Get this bitch out of here!" he screamed, leading her toward the front door as she struggled to keep up with the rather quick pace as he was pulling her locks. Turmoil ensued as the "boys" scrambled to assist trying to prevent too big of a scene. In just a few moments, a disheveled Elvis returned to the TV lounge, telling me apologetically, "Man, I'm sorry, I wasn't raised to treat a woman like that. She's crazy…I don't know what's wrong with her."

I felt silly as I blurted out, "I don't blame you, Elvis," thinking this was one of those "I don't believe this is happening" moments. He definitely wanted me to accept his apology. It was a Southern gentleman thing with conflicting emotions raging. Phone calls were hurriedly made, no bad publicity was wanted. I don't know if the Colonel was contacted, but in any event, within thirty minutes Christina returned. She and Elvis disappeared and the excitement was over.

Lamar had won the bet. Dorsey was out $300 and The Casuals soon left Hollywood dragging all our gear in a trailer behind the rental car. We would never party with "E" again, but every time one of his records would come on we'd start laughing and reliving that West Coast trip and the "wild night in Bel Air."

Bobby Russell

Bobby Russell, Steve Gibb, and Buzz with the coveted Grammy

And I wake up in the morning with my hair
down in my eyes and she says hi.
"Little Green Apples,"
by Bobby Russell

Just above the old Mom's Tavern, which is now Tootsie's Orchid Lounge in Nashville's lower Broadway, was an egg crate–walled monaural recording studio, originally owned by Joe Reavis and aptly called Reavis Recording. I will always be thankful for the people I met at that rat hole of a facility and the life-changing events that transpired in those early days of recorded music in Nashville long before there was a Music Row. One day at that studio, I met a guy who would take me to another level in music.

I don't recall exactly why Robert Lee "Bobby" Russell was at that same studio, which had changed ownership and was known as Fidelity. The studio was then owned by Kenny Marlow, a young attorney bitten by the rock-'n-roll bug and aspiring to be in entertainment law, and another fellow Vanderbilt student, Gary Walker from Missouri, who had already had some success as a writer, with cuts by Jim Reeves, Carl Smith, and Kitty Wells, all destined to become legends in country music.

Bobby had already recorded one song for Kenny, "The Raven" by The Impalas. He wrote the song and sang lead on the take-off of Edgar Allan Poe's classic poem. As fate would have it, we were both at Fidelity on that afternoon in '58 and struck up a friendship that would last until Bobby's death in 1992.

"Do you write?" Bobby abruptly asked after Kenny had introduced us.

"Oh yeah!" I quickly replied, having written at least a grand total of three or four things one might loosely refer to as actual songs. I figured that having written one half of a local hit with the Casuals qualified me to call myself a songwriter.

"Let's write one," he suggested. So, we booked the first of many writing appointments. We came from two different sides of town: he from upper-middle class Green Hills, and me from the more blue collar neighborhood of Inglewood. He attended Hillsboro High, referred to by us Littonites (Isaac Litton High School) as "tea sippers." We didn't let this slight cultural difference interfere at all with our burning desire to create music and the mutual goal of success in writing, publishing, and producing records. This rather arrogant, red-haired, ruddy-faced teenager intrigued me. I had not met anyone interested in songwriting with such confidence, and he definitely had a gift for writing. Bobby was the son of Frank and Ann Russell and it was in the living room of their home on Sperry Road, where we wrote our first song. I banged on the piano and Bobby played his sister Ginger's gut string guitar. (I don't think he ever owned a guitar of his own and wrote most of his hits on the one borrowed from Ginger.) We clicked! We quickly wrote "Tennessee," a "bop-a-ba-ba-ba"–sounding song in the style of California surfers Jan and Dean, who were recording for Los Angeles–based Liberty Records. I had a monaural Wollensak recorder we used to tape our early songs on and we immediately made a rough work tape so we could remember all the cool licks we had created. There's nothing like the birth of a new song. We were excited and ready to take "Tennessee" to the next level. Each new song has a life of its own and like our children we nurture them, prepare them, and finally release them. Like for any other offspring we are sometimes amazed at where they land and what becomes of them. Such was the case with this three-chord wonder, "Tennessee." Our beloved home state had become the title of our first professional co-write and it would soon open doors for us.

In that first writing session a dream was born for the two of us. We were hopeful and fearless, loving music, and anxious to get on with our writing. We looked forward to the day when we would have hits and be the owners of our own publishing company. There was no doubt we would make it. It was just a matter of when it would happen.

We were given a massive twenty-five–dollar budget to cut our first demo session. That amounted to five dollars per musician. Tony Moon played guitar for us. Richard, Bobby Watts, and I had met Tony while singing with Brenda at the famed Brooklyn Paramount Theatre's Murray "The K" Kaufman's Rock 'n Roll Show, which also featured The Coasters, Bo Diddley, and Little Anthony & the Imperials. Tony was appearing there with Dante & the Evergreens, performing their cover of

"Alley Oop." We really liked Tony and his guitar style, so we invited him to join The Casuals. Tony was ready for a change and in a few days had made the move from California to Tennessee.

A fellow classmate of Bobby's, Bergen White, was also on the session and he may have played bass on the song. I am positive, however, that he sang background vocals with us. Bergen, the son of a local Baptist music minister, would graduate from Belmont College and become one of Nashville's most prolific and successful arrangers and conductors. He always had great ideas to enhance a recording and certainly helped teach Bobby and me the art of harmony and its commercial importance to a song. When we were struggling with a vocal part he would hum each of our notes in our ears just prior to our singing entrance. Bergen immediately adapted to studio work and is now a highly sought-after background singer, performing on countless records and jingles, often subbing with the internationally acclaimed Jordanaires as well as conducting the orchestra for the annual Country Music Association (CMA) Awards television show.

With the promise of financial backing, we knew we had assembled the best five-dollar demo players in town and proceeded to have a fun time in the studio. I can't recall who the other musicians were on the session, but we often did most of the instruments ourselves. I had become a "tambourine specialist" since all the skilled positions were filled by much more talented players. There were no multitrack recording machines then, so we kept Kenny who also engineered, very busy going from one monaural machine to another adding anything we thought was cool to the track. Incidentally, Bergen later named his company "Cool Licks, Inc.," and he and I went on to sing many of those licks on countless sessions for many artists, working for several great and gifted producers of that era, including Bill Justis, Fred Foster, Ron Chancey, and Kelso Herston, to mention a few. These men not only hired us to sing, but listened to and recorded many of my and Bobby's songs during the next ten years or so.

What a kick it was for three guys fresh out of high school to be in a real studio cutting one of our songs! Equally thrilled with the first Russell-Cason recording effort was aforementioned Gary Walker, now associated with Lowery Music as a song plugger. He said, "Man, this sounds like a record, not just a demo!" We immediately envisioned our names on the record as not only writers but now as

producers. But wait, there was yet no record label. Gary, who now worked for Atlanta publisher Bill Lowery, was an aggressive salesman and always scurried about with a handful of scribbled notes with pitch ideas on them. He had a great smile accompanied by a high-pitched giggle that he would burst out with when he'd hear something he liked. Gary assured us he would present us as a recording act if we desired. Naturally, we gave him the quick go ahead. So before the tape had cooled, he was on the street with "Tennessee." He took the song to Paul Cohen, former A&R (artist and repertoire) chief of Decca Records who had started his own company, Todd Records. I'm not sure Paul understood what this "new sound" was all about, but he liked it and wanted to release it. Nowadays record people must be totally in love with a song or project to put it out. But fortunately for us these record renegades of the '60s and '70s took chances. Bobby and I were never afraid to be different, proven later by his unique and innovative lyrics on such songs as "Honey" and "Little Green Apples." So, our wacky combination of folksy country and West Coast rock 'n roll probably sounded as different as a rap record the first time you heard one. The bottom line was, Bobby and I had our first commercial release together as the hastily named group The Todds.

In those days songwriters took as many shots at success as possible, so with The Todds record that had been released not exactly burning up the airwaves, we actively pursued the idea of Jan and Dean covering us in doing their version of "Tennessee." Once again the services of our mentor, Gary Walker, came into play. Gary exemplified the title songplugger in the most positive and creative way I had seen and continue to see in the music business. Right in the middle of the country music, we had found a man with a rock-'n-roll heart. He had come to Nashville as a songwriter and had already had songs cut by Jim Reeves and others. Not only did he have a keen eye for marketing, but he was willing to delve into the rock and pop music of that time. That, in my opinion, made him a true visionary of his day. He was also a brave guy to put up with a couple of rather cocky and pushy kids like Bobby and me. Gary, only a year or so prior to meeting Bobby and me, was a proud writer of not one, but two songs, on the charts at the same time which was quite an accomplishment for a new writer. The songs were "According to My Heart" by Jim Reeves on RCA and "Repenting" by Kitty Wells on Decca.

Gary was a native of Missouri and had grown up loving all styles of music, including country, and while in college at South Central Missouri University, he began writing songs. During that time period of the '50s, country legend Red Foley was hosting a highly popular television show, The Ozark Jubilee, which originated in Springfield, Missouri. Gary virtually hung around the show, hoping to interest a singer in one of his songs. Carl Smith, whom I consider as the Alan Jackson of his day, recorded Gary's "Trademark," which emerged in 1999 on Sire Records by the highly talented Mandy Barnett, who was the last act the legendary Owen Bradley produced.

He didn't realize it at the time, but Gary would soon become a pioneer in what would eventually become the field of song plugging, an activity that took place on what was to become Music Row in Nashville. Gary's desire to earn his master's degree in history brought him to Nashville's Vanderbilt University where he met H. McKinley (Kenny) Marlow, a law student who was also an aspiring songwriter. In talking, they discovered their mutual love for songwriting and the new rock-'n-roll sound that was changing the sounds of all contemporary recording in virtually all fields of music. Both young men possessed entrepreneurial spirits, so when Kenny suggested they buy Reavis Recording Studio, the excitement and challenge began. It was a loan from Gary's father-in-law, Paul Boone, that led to the purchase of the studio which was located at 420 Broadway in a part of Downtown Nashville that went from being a retail furniture district to an entertainment strip for tourists. Broadway is now lined with small nightclubs and bars, catering to the country and alternative music fans.

"My father-in-law was impressed with Kenny," Gary recalled and the pair wasted no time in remodeling the tiny space. Under Kenny's supervision, the creation of an echo chamber was one of the first orders of business. In those days, there were very few electronic or digital reverb units in operation in studios. So live echo chambers or rooms were the ticket when one could not afford a German built EMT plate–style piece of equipment. Often, we as writers and singers would judge a studio mainly on its echo effects on the music we were laying down on tape. So the fact that the new Fidelity Studio had a juicy live echo sound really appealed to Bobby and me. I was still chasing "the dream" as a performer with The Casuals and hoping one day to become a solo artist on a strong pop-rock record label that might take a chance on a Southern white boy, who at times sounded a tad black. Looking back, I now realize I perceived my voice as being more rhythm-and-blues sounding than it actually was. Hooking up with Bobby had broadened my musical spectrum and initiated a serious approach to the art of songwriting. He introduced me to the idea of writing songs with more depth than I had ever attempted. He was the master lyricist of our era as would be proven by "Little Green Apples" and "Honey," among many of his songs. He also could play finger-style like Chet Atkins. Now that was cool.

Gary and Kenny had built a place to record rock music and it was a natural draw to performers coming to Nashville seeking to fulfill their dreams of seeing and hearing one of their songs on vinyl, the format for recorded music in the '50s. Among those who found their way to Fidelity were the Isle Brothers, Jimmy and Ron, from Illinois. Bobby and I greatly admired them. Oddly enough, Jimmy was a redhead like Bobby and even had that trademark blush when he was forced to look you in the eye to converse. Shyness is a misunderstood personality trait of many entertainers, and through the years as our partnership developed, I was often the business spokesman for our professional efforts.

"Man, they're on a hot New York label!" Bobby would say, referring to the Isles. Gary had placed one of Ron and Jimmy's master recordings with Sceptor/Wand Records, who had such acts as The Shirelles and Dionne Warwick. We just knew these two talented Yankees were going to be among the first artists to make it out of our pioneer group of rockers hanging out at Fidelity. You see, "making it" in the stardom sense never crossed our mind. Bobby and I simply wanted to be on the radio. Everything else would fall into place if that happened. Unfortunately for the Isles, the "big one" never came. Jimmy's song "Diamond Ring" was recorded as a follow-up to "How the Time Flies" by Jerry Wallace, a pop stylist who recorded for Challenge Records of Los Angeles. As in so many songs that follow hits, this one topped off in the eighties on the music charts. "We must have had thirty or forty of their songs cut," Gary recalled.

Although we were impressed by the action they were creating, Bobby and I didn't feel threatened by the Isles or our other local peers. We were optimistic enough about the future to believe our real

competitors were the guys and gals from L.A. and The Brill Building in Manhattan who already had hits under their belts. You must understand that solid killer singles were the kind of songs we were going for. In the '60s, there was no album project for an artist until they had that big single on the charts. Once again the influence of Al Nevins and Don Kirshner motivated us.

"Man, if we can get some assignment writing jobs or just do some custom-tailored songs for a particular artist we'll have smash records," Bobby speculated. During this period of my career, I was wearing several hats: working with the band full time, singing background vocals on demo and master recording sessions, and writing with Bobby. Bobby and I had differences over the years, but we always agreed that had it not been for Gary, we would have not made it in the business. There is a distinct difference between many of the songpluggers of today and Gary in that he not only knew how to cast and present a song, but he had a passion for a song and that enthusiasm carried over to the artist or producer to whom he was pitching.

Bobby and I continued to write when I was not on the road. Gary became a publisher for Lowery Music of Atlanta and published our next "ba-ba-ba" Jan and Dean–type song, "Popsicle." We made another Todds single on the tune "Popsicle," which, like "Tennessee," was later covered by Jan and Dean on Liberty. The Todds' session was produced by our new production company, Tri-Arts, which Bobby and I formed with Tony Moon. The three of us opened an office together on 16th Avenue, but soon realized we had no viable way to pay rent. Tony and I were barely getting by financially on our gig money and Bobby was receiving a twenty-five-dollars-a-week draw from Painted Desert Music, where Gary was then working. Lack of funds, however, never discouraged us. We managed to raise money to do "Popsicle" as The Todds and "Watermelon," using the name The Countdowns, on Kenny's Image label and "She Has" by the F.J. Babies. All records featured the three of us on vocals and many of the instruments. That Tony was a fine rock and blues guitarist helped tremendously in the studio. The "F.J" on the "She Has" disc stood for Felton Jarvis, the personable head of the ABC record label in Nashville and the record came out on the APT label, a subsidiary of ABC. We simply ran out of group names and Felton obliged! What fun we had in those days, always writing and planning the next production, hoping one would hit. They never did, but we were learning. Bobby's writing was getting stronger with every song. It was also during this time period, when Tony and I wrote "Lay Down Your Arms (Soldier of Love)," which Noel produced on Arthur Alexander and was released on Capitol in the '90s as part of The Beatles, Live at the BBC CD. Marshall Crenshaw cut it in the '80s, and Pearl Jam used it as a B-side in 1999 and on the "No Boundaries" compilation CD. Tony and I have had many a laugh over the fact this song has never hit as a single, but sure has earned well for us.

From the beginning, Bobby and I dreamed of owning our own publishing company. We didn't know how we would pull it off, but we were determined to do it. I had started to get a few sessions as a background singer and Bobby's writing was getting better with each song when suddenly our lives changed. Our plans were instantly put on hold when I was offered a deal I couldn't very well turn down. I had always wanted to give L.A. a try, maybe to study film direction at the Pasadena Playhouse, but this was a "for real" new job in the sun and fun of California.

Bobby was a constant source of inspiration to me. He challenged me to write a more complete and unique lyric. While the right words for me were hard to come by, neither of us ever seemed to struggle with the melodies, having both been rooted in so many styles of music: church music, some classical training, obviously country influences, the golden era of pop songs and stylists, and ultimately—the genres that jumpstarted our teenage years—rhythm and blues and rock 'n roll. But Bobby had something the rest of us renegade garage-band combo members didn't have. He had a gift for putting powerful

emotions into a song, enhanced by an uncanny talent for rhyme and he could transcend the poetic with everyday language and touch your heart. Later on, his masterpieces—"Honey," "Little Green Apples," and "The Night the Lights Went Out in Georgia"—would affirm the art he so effortlessly produced.

Go West, Young Man: The Hollywood Dayze

Garry Miles, ready for "The Coast"

Someday we'll remember how it used to be,
There's not a thing that life can bring
As much to me as 1963.

"1963" written by Buzz Cason,
Snuff Garrett, and Cliff Crofford.
Recorded by Bobby Vee.

In the '60s, the Black Poodle Lounge and Showbar was a nightclub unique to Nashville in that it featured rock 'n roll. It was located in the city's famed Printer's Alley, a colorful little strip of nightlife known for its restaurants, jazz clubs, and strip clubs. The colorful "Skull" Schulman owned and operated the famous venue The Rainbow Room, where the top burlesque acts available usually appeared. Skull, also owned the Poodle, and walked his large contingency of toy poodles down the Alley every afternoon. He always dressed in outlandish outfits and dyed the dogs' hair weird colors entertaining the throngs of tourists who visited there nightly. You could get it all in the Alley: jazz, blues, strippers, good food, and the "new kids on the block," the boys who played rock 'n roll!

By this time, The Casuals had become known as more than just Nashville's first rock band. We even had "America's Top Show Band" painted on our shiny black trailer towed by our equally shiny black station wagon (pre-tourbus days), which we purchased new yearly due to the 100,000 plus miles we put on a vehicle annually. They loved us in the Alley. By 1962, we had about four real hot forty-five–minute sets, including two show sets with artist imitations and our most requested tunes. Tony Moon was our lead guitarist at that time, having replaced Wayne Moss who had left the band to become a session player. Tony was a good showman (a requirement in a group like ours), but also had a knack for songwriting.

We would finish our gig at one or two in the morning depending on the crowd and the night of the week. Jimmy Washer, a co-owner of an after-hours club and a professional gambler, frequently stopped in to see our show and had befriended us. He was an extremely nice man, always dressed in a suit and tie. I guess he realized how broke musicians usually were, so he extended a standing invitation to us to stop by his place, the Uptown Club, to relax and have a steak on him. Now this was music to the ears of our usually hungry bunch. We couldn't afford to eat out often, much less to drink or gamble. But Jimmy didn't care. Per his instructions, we told the inquiring eye that peered through the tiny speakeasy-style window at the club who we were and we were admitted in. We would stay an hour or so, have a nice meal, watch the craps table, and then leave. No strings attached. Jimmy just liked us, not unlike so many others of that era who were kind to us by hiring us repeatedly and treating us like family.

On this particular winter night, we were having a juicy filet and looked up to see the familiar face of a young man rolling dice. It was Snuff Garrett, who paused briefly to introduce me to his boss, Al Bennett, president of Liberty Records. Although I had recorded for Liberty, I had never met Al. Both men were intent at the game at hand, so I pulled back to let them play. I learned later in L.A. just how much the Liberty Records gang loved to gamble.

In his distinct Texas drawl, Snuff said, "Hold on a minute, Buzzer, I want to ask you somethin'." As I leaned a little bit closer he blurted out, "Ever thought about movin' to California?" Not knowing what he was getting at, I told him how California, Hollywood in particular, had been a part of my original showbiz dreams and how I wanted to be behind the scenes in films, possibly working eventually as a director.

Without hesitation he quickly asked, "How'd ya like to come to L.A. and work as my assistant and learn to produce and do some acts for me?"

I was startled and wondered how serious he was. "Well, that would be great, I'll, uh, let you know about that," I muttered, not too keen on letting the rest of the band hear this conversation.

"Real soon," Snuff replied, his face in a smirk that I would soon become accustomed to seeing.

"How soon?" I asked.

"Tomorrow morning," he shot back.

EVERLASTING LOVE • 75

"Aw, Snuff, come on, you've got to be kiddin'!" I said in obvious shock over the unreasonable timeframe.

"That's just a few hours away," I protested, hoping he would cut me a little slack on the deal. However, having previously worked with Snuff, I was aware of his stubbornness and assumed he wanted a prompt decision.

"I've got an early flight, so call me at the hotel and let me know," he ordered.

"OK," I said, shaking his hand and quickly shouting a "good night" to the boys in the band, excited, but not ready to share the news of this offer which would not only affect the group I had started out with, but could change my life in a dramatic way. I drove my little VW bug home, woke up my wife, Rose, and announced, "Guess what? We're moving to California."

Dub Allbritten, Brenda Lee's manager, had also served as my personal manager during my brief stint as a one-hit–wonder recording artist and was rather surprised that I had actually landed a paying job in the record company end of the music business. He had previously tried to assist me in renegotiating my record contract as an artist with Liberty, the same record label that I was going to work for.

Snuff had shown to me for the first time his stubborn and almost ruthless business tactics when he declared, "Buzzer, I'll sit on your contract if you don't go along with us!" I had requested to be paid as a solo artist on my Garry Miles records rather than splitting the royalties three ways as part of The Statues, the trio that Hugh Jarrett had put together with Richard Williams and me. It turned out to be a moot point since my follow-up records had flopped and The Statues were dropped from the label. On the California decision, Dub quickly advised me what to ask in the way of salary and assured me The Casuals would go on as a band and continue to back up Brenda with or without me. I had previously turned down an offer from our former booking agent, X. Cosse, husband and manager of gospel music great Martha Carson, to move with them to the West Coast. He wanted to develop me as a solo artist. He proposed sending me to all the acting schools, landing a record deal, and attempting to run me through the star system, whatever that was. I did not accept because he wanted me to leave my wife and daughter behind most likely for good, since it was not cool for teen idols to be married in their early career as they sought fame. Moreover, I was more interested in writing, producing, and publishing by then. "If this is what you want to do, you should pursue it," Dub advised. Within a few days, I was on a plane bound for California.

After locating an apartment on Sepulveda Boulevard in the lovely San Fernando Valley community of Sherman Oaks, I moved the family westward in the VW with a luggage rack on top. When we reached the winds of West Texas, we were almost blown off the highway, the famed old Route 66. On the last leg of the journey that included a night drive through the Mojave Desert, crossing the mountains and looking down at the sea of L.A. lights, I realized it was a pinnacle moment in my life and career as Rose, my daughter, Tammy, and I arrived in a city I had dreamed of living and working in.

We lived thirty minutes from Hollywood and 6920 Sunset Boulevard where Liberty was located. I enjoyed the drive in every morning, usually with the top down on the little Chevy Two I had bought from Liberty jazz producer Tommy LiPuma, who now produces the popular Diana Krall. I could see the crews filming Wagon Train on the hillsides, where Universal City is now located. Southern California was beautiful in the early '60s and the San Fernando Valley still had a few small ranches and orange groves scattered around, like the one across from us out in Panorama City where we would later live.

The first night I was in Tinsel Town, I went to my first session at the studio, where I would spend many hours during the next two years. It was Bill Putman's United Recorders, a complex of state-of-the-art studios used by the top artists and record companies of the day as well as many of the hot film and commercial producers. I had recorded there one time previously, singing on "Dream Girl," the flop follow-up to "Look For A Star," written by Steve Venet, brother of Nick Venet who signed The Beach Boys to Capitol Records. My one session had been in '60. This was '62, and it was a thrill to meet The Crickets. On that initial record date I sat in on, the Texas boys were backing Bobby Vee on the Bobby Vee Meets The Crickets album. Along with the leader and drummer, Jerry Allison, were Sonny Curtis, Glen D. Hardin, and lead vocalist Jerry Naylor. Snuff was the producer, and after the session, he introduced me to Bobby and the guys. We all hit it off well, and from that night on, the whole crew took me under its wing and we had many fun hours of work together. Snuff quickly assigned Buddy Knox to me as my first artist to produce and not long after that, with Jerry Allison's approval, he gave me the chance to cut a hit on The Crickets. I admired and respected both of these acts and immediately went to work seeking material for them.

"When we work, we work. When we play, we play," declared Snuff, my new boss and mentor at Liberty. The two years I would spend there became a crash course in every facet of the commercial music business. Before Snuff had come to Nashville to produce our group, The Statues, for Liberty, I had met him briefly at the radio station in Lubbock, Texas, where he raved about Buddy Holly and The Crickets. He interviewed us that night as we plugged our record on Dot. I had seldom seen such enthusiasm from a radio personality. After a short stint as a deejay, Snuff would receive a call from Don Blocker of Liberty, urging him to come to California to work as the local promotional man for the label. Snuff didn't make much money in his early Hollywood days and even slept in his car behind the record company for awhile. It didn't take him long to work his way into producing and the young Texan would soon become a virtual tycoon in the pop and rock record business. I would soon discover his energetic, professional drive was unlike anything I'd ever seen.

Liberty was located on 6920 Sunset Boulevard, which was the home of Gene Autry's Republic Pictures in the '40s and early '50s. This was a kick for me since Gene was my favorite cowboy as a child. Our offices were right in the heart of Hollywood, located directly across from Hollywood High School. It was a fun place to work and almost everyone on staff there who was cutting their teeth in the record business at that time would later become successful in the music industry. The second floor of the ranch-style building housed most of our staff producers and the A&R staff. My little cubbyhole was sandwiched between Texan Tommy Allsup, who headed up our country division, on my left and Snuff to my right. Tommy was a talented guitarist, who was also the musician's contractor for all of Snuff's record dates. He was an expert on Western swing and was friends with all the greats in that field, including Bob Wills. I was thrilled when Tommy asked me and a group to sing on a Wills album. The other two singers in the session were Vikki Carr and Billy Mize. Vikki recorded for Liberty and was gaining a strong following as a pop singer. Billy was a well-known West Coast country singer. We had fun doing that record. At one point, Tommy politely told Wills that he had "skipped a beat" in

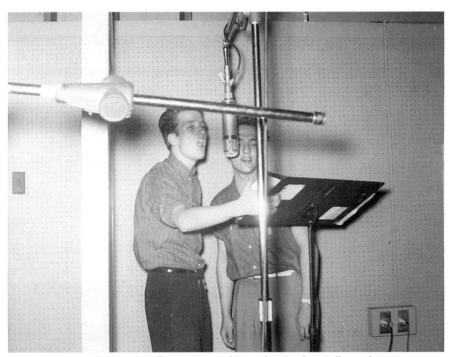

Buzz and Richard Williams at United Recorders Studios Hollywood, 1960

one of the songs. Wills quickly replied, "Son, I've been skippin' them meters for years, and it ain't hurt my career none yet!"

Bob Reisdorf's Dolton Records occupied the west wing of the second floor. He was the founder and producer of The Fleetwoods, The Ventures, and Vic Dana, all hit acts with big sales figures and was a pioneer of the Seattle music scene. Our head of A&R, Don Blocker, pretty much approved whatever Snuff desired, which wasn't bad for those of us "in" with Snuff. He was also the same guy that Snuff deferred to when it was time to fire Tommy, Ed Silvers, who was A&R in New York, and myself. But until that event, which fell under the "budget cutting" category, we sure had lots of fun making music and spending the company's money in the true rockin' American fashion.

A typical day for me at the record company consisted of listening to songs submitted by publishers from all over the world and making appointments with L.A., New York, and Nashville songpluggers that Snuff couldn't get to. I was young, enthusiastic, and hungry for a hit song. After listening to a room full of songs that had been sent as demos on the old acetate format, I only discovered one song I liked written by two unknown British songwriters, John Lennon and Paul McCartney.

I even saw a few walk-ins like the one our able assistant and all-around girl Friday, Annette Smerigan, announced one day, "He says he's from Cucamonga," she said.

"Cooca what?" I asked laughingly.

"His name is Frank Zappa," she said. With a name like that from a town like Cucamonga, I just had to see this guy. He wore a tight-fitting, tailored business suit and boots not unlike the outfits most of us wore to work back then. Yes, he was weird and his music was strange. But as it turned out, we talked as much about his divorce and how freaked he was about it as we did about music. Snuff and I liked two of his songs and produced them with Ricky Paige and me on the vocals. I don't think they were ever released, and it was years before I saw Frank again.

I spoke to him prior to a concert in Houston, where he recognized me from stage saying, "This is the second guy who's ever heard my songs in Hollywood." (Art Lebow of Original Sound Records was the first.) Frank played some incredible guitar that night and convinced me of his apparent genius.

My first session as a producer for Liberty was The Crickets' up-tempo remake of the Ray Charles classic "Lonely Avenue." We cut the tracks at United's Western Room, a smaller but good-sounding tracking room I came to love. Bones Howe was the engineer and always a delight to work with. Jerry Naylor did a spirited lead vocal, and I was pleased with the record that unfortunately only bubbled under the Hot 100 charts in Billboard magazine.

I was also assigned to produce another rock pioneer, Buddy Knox. He and I came to Nashville to record "Hitch Back to Georgia," a Joe South song. One of my favorite people and certainly one of the most talented men to ever pick up a guitar or play, sing, and write songs, Jerry Reed was on the session. Jerry played quite a few sessions before having his string of hits and a career as a successful actor that began not long after that date. These days, Jerry and I occasionally write songs and play golf together. Buddy and I also did a cover of Ernest Tubb's "Thanks a Lot." Both songs were released as singles on Liberty.

The first week I was at Liberty, Snuff told me, "Buzzer, get a group of guys together and I'll use you on all the background vocal sessions I can get you on. You can be the contractor on the dates too." What a bonus for me! I went about looking for singers. My search led me to a friend I had met in Nashville. Johnny "Dog" Mac-Crae, who was working with Gary S. Paxton at his rather infamous studio digs on Argyle Street, where "Alley Oop" and the "Monster Mash" records as well as hits by The Association and Tommy Roe were recorded. Much craziness surrounded that center of Hollywood rock 'n roll where the engineer stomped on the upstairs control room floor, signaling the musicians to start recording, but it would take at least another chapter to tell all the stories I've heard about the place. Johnny suggested I talk to Carol Lombard (no relation to the famed actress of the same name), who was an excellent singer. Carol introduced me to Ron Hicklin, Al Capp, and Bob Zwirn to sing with me on sessions, which resulted in our singing behind acts like Jackie DeShannon, Bobby Vee, and even as The Chipmunks (I was Alvin)! Ron, Al, and Bob had moved to California from Seattle and along with Stan Farber had cut one album for Capitol Records.

Ron would go on to be one of the top background singers on records and jingles in the L.A. area. He became successful enough to buy the old Hollywood Chamber of Commerce building in a prime location on Sunset Boulevard, where he built his HK Killer Music and produced, wrote, and sang on thousands of major radio and television commercials. He had also sung the harmony voices on all the Gary Lewis & the Playboys records.

Snuff occasionally allowed me to oversee a session when he was not available or double-booked. Ross Bagdasarian jumped on The Beatles bandwagon by easily talking Al Bennett and Snuff into The Chipmunks Sing The Beatles album. Along with the other singers, I stayed in the RCA studios for more than twelve hours straight cutting the Lennon-McCartney songs note-for-note at half the speed of the original versions. When we sped them up, it produced the high-pitched sound of the famed little critters. The album sold well, and later in the '80s, I worked with Ross, Jr. on Urban Chipmunk, which the younger Bagdasarian co-produced with Larry Butler, my good friend who was then producing monster hits with Kenny Rogers and other artists. Ross Jr. had carried on the Chipmunk concept after his father had died an untimely death in California in 1972.

One night we had finished backgrounds on a session orchestrated by the great arranger Ernie Freeman, who conducted strings and horns on countless hits for Snuff. It was a late-night date, and Snuff and Ernie had left me and the engineer to finish the day's work. The artist was Julie London, the beautiful singer-actress who had a hit with "Cry Me a River," written by her husband, Bobby Troupe. I had walked up to the Brown Derby to pick up some take-out orders and when I returned to RCA studios, the engineer Dave Hassinger had turned the lights off in the mailroom and only the music stand light was dimly glowing out in the area where Julie was singing. Dave was looking down at the soundboard, rather sheepishly.

"What's going on, Dave?" I asked.

"Oh, nothing. It just got a little warm for Julie, so she removed her sweater and I'm just tryin' not to stare in her direction…too much!" I spent two whirlwind years in California, and I sure learned a lot about making records and had tons of fun, especially that "bra only" incident.

Jan and Dean were heroes of mine, especially since they had recorded "Tennessee" and "Popsicle," which Bobby Russell and I had written. To finally meet them at the Liberty offices was a thrill for me. The duo had some of their biggest hits during the time I was at Liberty. I got to know Dean Torrence a little better than his partner, Jan Berry. Dean and I had an idea for a "John Lennon" cap and even had a prototype, but never got the project off the ground. I'll always be grateful for those guys breaking Bobby and me into the pop and rock record charts.

During that same timeframe I met a lanky piano player with a pompadour hairstyle. He was playing on a session for Lou Adler, who was producing Johnny Rivers at the time. I was impressed by the way he handled the rhythm section so effortlessly, telling each player what to play, how to play it, and when. Not long after that I had the opportunity to hear him jamming with the musicians after another record date. This time he sang with a mixture of a whiny country style laced with extremely soulful overtones. It turned out he was Leon Russell, and we've been friends ever since. Later on, I hooked him up with Snuff and they co-produced several Gary Lewis records together. After a few years of business conflicts and clashing egos, the two both declared they wished I had never introduced them to each other! Leon moved to the Nashville area in the '80s and I had fun cutting a few sides on him along with Brent Maher at my studio in Berry Hill. On a recent fall day, I recalled how Leon had "turned farmer" when he moved to Tennessee, buying property in nearby Gallatin, north of Nashville. The tractor I was riding on that October day had been bought at a farm equipment supply store Leon had suggested. He loved to operate tractors and other heavy equipment during his rural tenure. Not exactly the "Mad Dogs and Englishmen" image!

James Burton, who was elected to the Rock and Roll Hall of Fame in 2000, was working exclusively for Rick Nelson as a staff guitarist on his television show and records. As I recall, he was on a $250-a-week salary, which was pretty darn good in those days. He was bored, however, and yearned to have the freedom to play on records other than Rick's. That's where I came in. I had been asked to produce some surfing instrumental albums to capitalize on the popular California sounds of the day. We decided to take the idea a few steps further. I came up with the LP title Liverpool, Dragsters, Cycles and Surfing, which added cars, bikes, and The Beatles to the mix of hastily written songs. Someone in our circle of friends knew James and asked him if he would like to join the fun of these sessions, which also included Hal

Blaine, Tommy Allsup, and the rocker himself, Leon Russell. Leon also co-wrote a tune for the record. James swore us all to secrecy, knowing if Rick found out he might get fired. The sessions were fun, and the vinyl of that particular album is now a collector's item, selling for a lot more than it is worth! Rick never found out about James's moonlighting and the Louisiana-born picker continued to play those great solos and rhythm grooves for Rick and later on the road with Elvis and more recently, Jerry Lee.

At Liberty, we would have weekly A&R meetings, where each staff producer would present there current or future projects. Naturally, Snuff held his cards pretty close and was hesitant to reveal little if anything about what he was doing. My two acts were Buddy Knox, whose son, Michael is now a successful producer in Nashville, and my buddies, the Crickets. However I did get lots of acts pitched to me by managers and others . On one such occasion, I was invited down to United Recorders to meet with a group of young singers, a handsome bunch of boys ranging from about six to ten, who were appearing regularly on a network television show. They sang great, were extremely polite and personable, so I decided to bring the idea to our record company at the next weekly meeting. I had the idea to record them in a young Beach Boys style.

"No kids," was the general comments and Liberty turned them down. "How can we miss with these guys?" I argued. "With weekly appearances on the Andy Williams Show, we 're bound to sell tons of records on these kids." The answer was no. They would later be produced by my friend, Rick Hall at his F.A.M.E. studios in Alabama and have a huge hit which launched a huge career. They were the Osmond Brothers!

As Snuff had stated upon my arrival in California, we would have fun when we weren't working. On one weekend we took our wives up to the Ojai Valley Resort, north of Los Angeles. The trip was a little too costly for my limited budget, but I decided to make the best of it. At the time, Avnet Industries owned Liberty Records. Al Bennett and his partner, Sy Waronker, had done quite well financially on the sale. One of the buyers, Lester Avnet, was also at Ojai that weekend, and in a fairly drunken state, he entertained us with a diving exhibition at the pool and later on he showed off his horseback-riding talents at the stables. I didn't play golf back then, so except for the scenery and Avnet's antics, it was a boring trip. Unfortunately, Lester Avnet committed suicide by jumping out of a building in Beverly Hills, apparently suffering from heavy business stress and other problems.

I grew up loving anything motorized. I always regretted that Aaron Brown and I never got that little "Whizzer" motorbike put together in his garage on Ardee Avenue since I longed for some kind of motorcycle. I guess that's why I loved delivering prescriptions on that sluggish old Cushman motor scooter. Snuff was friends with Don Everly whom I hadn't seen in awhile when we went to see him at his Hollywood Hills home one Saturday morning. Don owned a motorcycle he rarely ever rode. Snuff asked if I could use it and Don said OK, probably not realizing the abuse

I would put the bike through jumping dirt terraces being landscaped into that area at the time. Man! We did have fun and I managed to somehow return the bike unharmed. Then came fast cars and my desire to race them. Riverside, California, located just east of Los Angeles in the then near barren edge of the desert, was where I first got hooked on sports car racing. Snuff left me his new V8-powered Buick Riviera one weekend, so I sped out to Riverside from the Los Angeles Times Grand Prix to see the likes of Jim Clark, Roger Penske, Parnelli Jones, and many other great drivers compete.

I loved the road-racing atmosphere, and after moving back to Nashville, I bought my own race car and wound up driving for about twenty years. Carroll Shelby, a California race car builder, had built the Ford-based Cobra and "Hey Little Cobra," a hit by the Rip Chords, had been co-written by Carol Conner. Carol was an attractive young L.A. girl who had sung with the Phil Spector–produced group The Teddy Bears, hit makers of "To Know Him Is to Love Him." She came to see me at Liberty with an idea that if we wrote a song about Ford's upcoming affordable sports coupe, the Mustang, we might get a free car out of it. She had managed to acquire a free Cobra from Shelby based on the song's success. We wrote the Mustang song, I got to drive the Cobra rather rapidly through the Hollywood streets and alleys, but the free Mustang never happened. Carol and I wrote a couple of songs for movies, including one for Howard Hawks's racing film, *Red Line 7000*. For me it was a great thrill to meet the man who had directed Sergeant York and to sit in his office, which was decorated in the style of another of his films, *Hatari*. Mr. Hawks leaned back in his cane chair and very slowly and in great detail told us the story of the picture we were to compose the song for and precisely where it would go. We hastily wrote "Wildcat Jones", which Mr. Hawks approved of, and to this day, I receive modest royalties from performances of the tune on television.

Working with Snuff was not only highly educational for me, but it was also a lesson in human relations. While Snuff's business tactics were borderline ruthless at times, he possessed qualities in his business life that I admired and have been influenced by over the years. Among these attributes were his love for people and the music, and his natural and uncanny gift for picking a hit song. For example, he once spotted a title on a lead sheet in the trash and pulled it out, listened to the demo and cut a smash on it with Gene McDaniels. The song was "Hundred Pounds of Clay." He had the tenacity and drive to get things done his way, persuasive negotiating skills, the ability to put a record together in the two- and three-track recording days, and a zany sense of humor. He had quite a business head on him and I marveled at all the deals he constantly pursued. "I've gotta call Jack on this one," he would shout, referring to his business advisor, when we were

brainstorming a new idea. His intense quest for investments and other business opportunities inspired me to look outside the music industry for my financial future. He also reinforced my belief that copyrights are "where it's at" in our business. Since those days, I've been blessed to work with countless gifted, creative people, who have affirmed that owning your own music can be fulfilling and at times rewarding. Above all, Snuff went about it all in style and with a showbiz flair.

My two years in the Golden State went by quickly, and time does fly when you're young and having fun like we were, both at work and at play. After touring with The Crickets for awhile, I was back in Nashville checking out job possibilities. Had I not had a family to support, I would have happily joined a band and hit the road again doing what I loved, entertaining. During that time of the decision I set up a little office in Hollywood with Bob McCluskey, a songplugger who also managed Ray Peterson. I believe God puts certain people in your life to be there for you at crucial times like I was facing then. Bob was most helpful by providing a place where I could work. Had I stayed in California I would have continued to have been a part of Ron Hicklin's vocal group, which would become very successful doing session work. But I felt it was time to go home and the thought of raising a family in California seemed a bit too challenging at the time. I had lived the West Coast part of my dream.

I had experienced a whirlwind West Coast rockin' ride from the summer of '62, which also was the year that Ronald Reagan joined the Republican party through the sad day in November '63, when JFK was assassinated, to the memorable invasion of America by The Beatles in '64—a series of events that shaped our nation's future both socially and politically in dynamic ways.

I've always had hopes that my children and grandchildren would have similar gold rush desires like I had. It may not be California, but a place their hearts long to see. I pray they seek divine guidance in all they set out to do and pursue their goals with great passion.

A few years later, after I had moved back to Nashville, Bobby Russell and I were in Hollywood on business and went out one night to see Bonnie and Delaney Bramlett playing in a club in the Valley. Leon Russell was also in that band at the time. After the last set, everyone went to an after-hours place, the Plantation, where musicians and several hangers-on basically went to party, drink, and smoke dope 'til the wee, wee hours. I didn't like drugs or being around them, but I was stuck because Bobby and I had come together and he was having a good time. I wasn't.

Bobby Keyes, the sax player who wound up playing for The Rolling Stones for years, asked if I'd listen to this guy Charlie's songs. I reluctantly agreed and not being in a good mood to begin with, just listened to a few bars of each song. And unlike the way I would ever want to treat anyone I said, "Sounds like crap to me," looking at Charlie with his glazed-over eyes. I then stormed out of the room and waited outside until Bobby was ready to leave.

About a year later, Bobby and I were back in California, this time walking down Sunset Strip when Bobby Keyes stopped us on the sidewalk. After hellos and stuff, he asked, "Y'all remember that night at the Plantation when Buzz was listening to that guy Charlie's songs?"

"Sure," we answered in unison. "Well, that Charlie was none other than Charles Manson!" It was a hot day in Los Angeles, but when I heard that, a sudden chill ran through me.

Celebrity Snapshots

"**YOU'RE IN IT FOR** the pictures," songplugger Billy Martin, gazing at the "Wall of Shame" of photos at Creative Workshop, our studio in Berry Hill, Tennessee

I guess there's some truth to that statement, spoken in jest by my friend and co-worker. Money definitely wasn't the motivation to be in showbiz or more specifically, the music industry. The green stuff was scarce the first few years of my career. Undaunted by the challenge and hardships of breaking in, I pressed on, seeking hit records. I recently reflected on the past forty plus years and realized my journey, like so many we face in life, has continually been uphill, but one filled with hope and anticipation of another exciting project on the horizon. It can't get much better than that. Recently, I've experienced one of my more active years as a writer-publisher. Martina McBride's recording of "Love's the Only House," co-written with the outstanding writer Tom Douglas, capped off a great 1999. The following vignettes about various entertainers are some of my favorite quotes and snapshots. I have been truly blessed to have come in contact with so many interesting and gifted people!

The Chipmunks

That's right. I was "Alvin" of Ross Bagdasarian's famed Chipmunks on three occasions. My good friend Dickey Lee loves to annoy me by informing those who don't know that I was in fact one of the audio characters on three Chipmunks recordings. It's not that I'm embarrassed about it, but it's mainly because it takes several minutes to answer the usual "how di ya'll git them little fellers to sound like 'at?" We sure had fun doing the records, and I share more about being Alvin in other sections of this book.

Jackie Wilson

Jackie was probably the greatest black male soul-pop performer I have ever worked with. In 1959, appearing in Chicago at the MOA (Music Operators of America) Convention was a definite boost to a recording artist's career by facing the nation's top jukebox distributors and owners gathered in the Windy City to have fun, see the new equipment, and to hear some music by a select few of the industry's top acts. Brenda Lee's manager, Dub Allbritten, booked her and our band, The Casuals, for the feature show of the event, and naturally we were excited about appearing on the same stage with Jackie. The audience went wild over the rousing performances by Jackie and Brenda, and in his dressing room after the show, we were all still in a frenzy over the crowd's response. Everyone was jubilant over the success of the evening. It had been unadulterated good old rock 'n roll and R&B at their finest. Jackie, who was having his back rubbed by a lovely female assistant, made the night for us Southern rockers when he declared, "Me and Brenda and them boys tore 'em up out there!"

Frank Sinatra

One would rightfully ask what the greatest pop crooner of all time is doing in a book that is basically about rock 'n roll. Regardless, here's my little story about Ol' Blue Eyes. It was 1963. I was working for Snuff Garrett at Liberty Records at the time. Western Studio was owned by Bill Putnam and the highly successful United Recorders and was a favorite place of everyone to record. I was in the tiny control room of studio C, relaxing on the sofa in front of the recording console waiting for Snuff to arrive. Ron Hicklin and I were preparing to do background vocals. Directly behind us was one of the hottest teen idol rock singers of the day, Bobby Vee, who was also doing vocals that night on the session for Liberty Records. Next to Bobby was Bones Howe, the noted engineer who would later become a successful producer for acts, including The Fifth Dimension. We were all having a cup of coffee, joking around and wondering where Snuff was…then Frank Sinatra walked in! That's right, the Chairman of the Board himself! Our mouths fell wide-open, rendering us foolishly speechless. I glanced over my shoulder to confirm that Bobby and Bones were in shock, and indeed, they were.

"Oh I'm sorry fellahs, I'm supposed to be rehearsing somewhere here tonight… I guess I got the wrong room," Mr. Sinatra said rather politely.

There was still silence from behind the board, so I jumped up and told him, "Yes, sir, we're doing some overdubs in here tonight. You must be down the hall," referring to a studio at the end of the corridor just outside studio C.

"I'm sorry to disturb you guys," Sinatra quickly replied. About that time, Bones spoke up, offering to show the great crooner the studio, where it turned out he was warming up with his piano player for a benefit in honor of Nat King Cole who had recently passed away. An event was being held at the Palladium, just a block or so away. It was definitely a nutty way to meet one of the superstars of all time. Later, I tiptoed down the hall and listened outside the studio as he warmed up those "velvet pipes" and told myself over and over, "No, it would not have been cool to ask him for his autograph for my mom!"

Martin Luther King, Jr.

In 1968, the National Association of Television and Radio Artists, an organization of black broadcasters, convened in Atlanta. A handful of white producers and independent record label owners rather boldly attended the meeting with the primary intent to meet music directors and popular R&B deejays in order to get their records played. I had always dreamed of being a part of the blues music I had heard on that little red crystal radio on Ardee Avenue, and thanks to the combined efforts of a handful of Southern white boys and a few talented black singers bonded together by the love of the music, my dreams had become a reality.

I was in this elite group along with my partner, Bobby Russell. We owned two small labels and had recently released recordings by several black artists. Also in attendance at the event were Dan Penn and Chips Moman, who both were producing and writing in Memphis; Rick Hall from FAME Studios in Florence, Alabama; and Marshall Seahorn, the partner of successful writer-producer Allen Toussaint from New Orleans. The music trade publications were always invited to these type of meetings and Record World magazine had sent its Nashville editor, John Sturdivant, who incidentally was an ex–saxophone player and popular character along Music Row.

Although no one else in our group was interested, John and I decided to attend the keynote address by the Rev. Martin Luther King, Jr. The banquet and speech were held in the main ballroom of the hotel and somehow John and I managed front-table seats directly across from the podium. When it came time for Dr. King's address, these two kids from Inglewood, born into the eye of the racial storm of those times and lovers of soul music, were fired up and ready to hear—what was always the case with Dr. King—a fiery sermon that inspired, moved, and called the audience to the cause of peaceful social change. The crowd amened and applauded as Dr. King's delivery crescendoed to the dramatic and profound, "Free at last, free at last, great God Almighty, I'm free at last!"

We were on our feet instantly and were among the first to show our support for the great leader. We would have marched with him that night. It was a powerful feeling! But as I reached across the linen-covered table to shake the hand of this American hero, who would soon lose his life in Memphis, a huge man next to me turned over Dr. King's full glass of red wine, spilling the deep red beverage on his white cuff. John and I both managed to shake his hand, but I'll always think, judging by the startled look in Dr. King's eyes, he thought that rather than the big man next to me, it was I who ruined that nice dress shirt. We may have been the only whites in the audience, but we were as moved as anyone there. I was recently able to share with my kids and grandkids on Martin Luther King Day how I had shaken hands with the man himself.

Jerry Lee Lewis

Our band first opened for Jerry Lee at a concert in '58 in Richmond, Virginia, which was an eye-opener for us in that we got our first taste of early rock-'n-roll rowdiness. Notice I don't refer to it as violence since the events surrounding this particular first show with The Killer involved incidents meant for fun. We experienced our first and only egging onstage. This old theatrical audience participation practice included not only the throwing of eggs at an act they didn't like but also various vegetables, like tomatoes. I'll

The "Killer"

never forget the look on Johnny McCreery's face as the yellow of an egg flowed down the pickboard of his new Fender Stratocaster guitar. He was horrified and not long after this event quit the road forever. After the show, Jerry Lee and his band amused themselves by stomping on the roof of the brand-new '58 Buick Roadmaster they had just purchased to travel in. There they were out behind the theatre: Jerry, Roland Janes, and Russell P. Smith with cowboy boots on, dancing away.

In rare photo with "The Killer", Jerry Lee Lewis at after a show in 1958 at Tullahoma, TN. Left to Right Jerry King, (The Casuals' manager), Jerry Lee and Buzz.

A year or so later, we followed Jerry and the boys to Buffalo, New York. Jerry had decided we all needed a little side trip to see Niagara Falls. The small two-vehicle entourage pulled up to the stone wall overlooking the world-famous Horseshoe

Falls. Jerry jumped out of his car and up onto the wall. After gazing for no longer than thirty seconds, he threw back his shoulders with his blond curls flowing in the wind and declared, "Jerry Lee has seen the Niag-ah Falls. Now let's go, boys!"

Many more fun days with that particular crew would follow, but these were two events that will always stand out in our rock-'n-roll memories.

In 2006, I drove up to Owensboro, Kentucky with my son, Parker and original Casuals drummer and now booking agent, Billy Smith. The occasion was to see Jerry Lee perform at the Executive Inn, once a plush showplace where numerous top entertainers had appeared, The showroom, as it were, had been relocated to a large meeting room in the lower level of the hotel. I wanted Parker to see this true pioneer of rock 'n roll and since Parker had played piano since he was two, the show held a particular fascination to him. When we were touring with him, myself and the other Casuals would stand in the wings and never miss a note of Jerry's sets. That night, we would see a different "Killer", a toned down and more subdued musician, but still a man projecting that rockin' Memphis spirit.

As he moved slowly to the grand piano and his band vamped him on, Jerry reminded me of the little old man character that Tim Conway used to play on the Carol Burnett Show. About thirty minutes before the show, I had spoken to Jerry's long time guitarist, Kenny Lovelace and asked if we might speak to Jerry for a few minutes either before or after the show. Kenny shook his head, apologized and told us Jerry wasn't feeling well. It showed up in his sluggish movements but not in his boogie-style piano playing and strong vocals. "Son, you're looking at an old rocker making about $3000.00 a song,!"I whispered to Parker as Jerry lit into songs from his "Last Man Standing" album. Billy had estimated that The Killer would most likely receive about $30,000 for the performance, resulting in the per song figure I had arrived at, considering Jerry only played about ten songs. As Jerry rambled through "Mexicali Rose," I leaned over to songwriter Glen Sutton , who had written one of Jerry's biggest country hits, "What Made Milwaukee Famous," and told him "He's got about four decades to go before he gets to your song!" Jerry left off many of hits, including Glen's, and rolled on to his rousing closer, "Whole Lotta Shakin' Goin' On," which brought the crowd to its feet.

I once asked Russell P. Smith, Jerry's drummer what the Killer meant when he would yell out "drive, drive!" The skinny, always nervous Russell P. fired back, "He means to raise the tempo gradually." From then on I felt I had been given a "rock 'n roll secret," one used by one of the all time greats that would invarably "drive" the fans to the peak of excitement and into a frenzy, and as all the legendary entertainers do.......leave 'em wantin' more!

Gary S. Paxton

One of the true characters to ever sing, write, or produce a record is the zany and extremely talented Gary Paxton. The S, which stood for Sanford, was added after imposters tried to claim some of his royalties early in his career. (I would like one day to write a screenplay on this fascinating individual, but at this moment I will share a couple of crazy things I witnessed.) On the night I met him, Gary was shooting out streetlights behind the auditorium in Shreveport, Louisiana, where we both appeared on a rock-'n-roll show that night. I was appearing as Garry Miles with my one hit, and he was lead singer of the Hollywood Argyles of "Alley Oop" fame. When I asked him what in the world he was doing, he flashed that devilish grin of his and assured me it was all in fun and he and his boys got easily bored on the road so they always carried BB guns with them. Sometime later on the same tour, Bobby Rey, the sax player with the Argyles, fell flat on his back and was lying on the stage apparently unconscious.

Myself and several other Casuals gathered around concerned about the fallen musician's condition when Gary, who was kneeling by him looked up and said, "He's been takin' some stuff."

Someone in our group mentioned the dangers of a young man getting messed up with drugs and alcohol. Almost instantly, Bobby, who couldn't have been over twenty years old at the time, suddenly awoke to declare, "Man, I've been doin' pills and whisky for ten years and it ain't bothered me none yet!"

Carl Perkins

Probably the single most influential singer-writer-musician I ever listened to the rockabilly legend Carl Perkins. I was able later to meet and, praise the Lord, work with him. Those yellow Sun 45-rpm records and the rare 78 ones are treasures in any fan's collection. Although I possess a very few of his original discs, I am and always will be a fan. In addition to "Blue Suede Shoes," Carl's "Boppin' the Blues," "True Love," "Dixie Fried," and "Honey Don't" are all solid rock classics.

The Casuals first worked a show with Carl and his band in Cookeville, Tennessee. "If you boys ever get down to Jackson, pull right up in th' yard with that big ol' station wagon and come on in the house, don't need to knock, ya'll just head for th' kitchen an' getcha somethin' to eat… If ya' wanna smoke, that's ok, stomp out th' butts on th' floor if ya' want to!" That's the kind of guy Carl was, although he may have exaggerated the hospitality. A loving, caring, and spiritual man, Carl had a heart for fellow musicians, never placing himself above others, including our band, who stood in awe of this great Southern gentleman and architect of rock 'n roll. One night from

*Perry Potts, Billy Smith, Buzz, Johnny McCreery, Richard Williams,
and the great Carl Perkins, 1958*

*Carl Perkins and Buzz outside of Creative Recording in Berry Hill, Tennessee.
Note the "Suede" license tag.*

the stage of a small nightclub in Atlanta, he recognized me and my friend and a fellow songwriter—the highly talented Columbia recording artist Freddy Weller, formerly of Paul Revere & the Raiders—and managed to make us appear to be the stars of the moment rather than himself. In the late '80s, we saw each other outside a

Nashville studio and he declared, "I saw you up there on TV man and y'all was doin' it!" He was referring to my appearance in TNN with my rockabilly band, BC and the Dartz. He was always warm, friendly, and encouraging to all he came in contact with.

In 2010, after hearing a most unusual voice on a CD that came in the mail from Georgia, I started working on a record with the twenty three year old Jesse Couch, the young man who sang in such a unique, yet retro style. His guitar playing reminded me so much of Carl. I thought to myself, "this kid could singlehandidly revive the rockabilly sound, yet with a new twist."

Jesse is so great to write and record with, I recently turned to my longtme engineer and friend, Joe Funderburk and remarked, "I know there's a God 'cause He sent Jesse for me and you to work with!"And I know Carl would love hearing him play and sing.

Bo Diddley

When you mention pioneers of rock 'n roll, you can't leave out Ellas McDaniel, known to millions of fans as Bo Diddley. How many recording artists do you know who have hit songs titled after their own name? Such is the case of Bo, who recorded his personal anthem, "Hey Bo Diddley," a rocker featuring his patented tremolo guitar lick, used on virtually all his up-tempo numbers.

One of my great thrills as a Casual was backing Brenda Lee at the Brooklyn Paramount Theater in New York during the Christmas show of 1958. Bo was on the show and decided a grand entrance would be thrilling for the screaming teenage crowd, an audience whipped to a frenzy prior to every act by popular deejay Murray the K. Bo stood on a chair offstage and envisioned a dramatic leap onto the near center stage just as the curtain would rise. His plan went afoul, however, when at the point of landing, he apparently twisted his ankle and came crashing down in a noisy heap, guitar and all. The curtain quickly came back down. Stagehands rushed to his aid and everyone was shocked and wondering what kind of condition Bo was in. His trusty shaker (maracas) player Jerome, was leaving the stage area, headed for the old Cadillac hearse the band traveled in.

Casual members Bobby Watts, Richard Williams, and myself managed to stop Jerome and ask, "Hey, man, how's Bo?"

Jerome sadly replied, "Bo sick!" Many years later I talked to Bo backstage at a Nashville nightclub, and he recounted how he and Eddie Van Halen encountered the law in Mississippi, Bo's home state. When the cop gave him a speeding ticket, Bo said, "They used 'trickulation' on us!" Whether in song or conversation, Bo Diddley always had a way with words.

Bobby Darin, Frankie Avalon, and George IV

Left to Right: Bobby Darin, Dick Biondi,Frankie Avalon, Bob Marcucci, Buzz, George Hamilton IV and Richard Williams in Youngstown, Ohio at Deejay Biondi's Record Hop" in 1957.

Dick Biondi was one of the most dynamic and influential deejays of the early rock era with a radio career that lasted from the late '50s on into the '80s. He was a super nice man, a real character and extremely talented at playing records kids loved as well as personally entertaining them on and off the air. One way he built his fan base, in addition to making extra money, was through teen dances known then as record hops. Record companies would fly the artists they were promoting into various cities, mainly in the East, for a series of these promotional events held usually at an area high school.

In the winter of '57, Richard Williams, my singing partner, and I set out to Youngstown, Ohio, with his '52 Ford filled with boxes and the 45-rpm release on Dot Records "My Love Song for You" by our group, The Casuals. We checked in the hotel designated by Biondi and our Dot promotion man and soon found ourselves in the company of future teen idol Frankie Avalon and his manager, Bob Marcucci. Bob quickly recruited us to sing behind Frankie at the evening events. We had brought red jackets for the shows that matched a similarly colored blazer Frankie planned to wear. After comparing complexion problems and applying the necessary Clearasil, we were off to the evening's rock-'n-roll adventures. We were all seventeen, two Southern boys and a South Philly kid, ready to take on the screaming frenzy awaiting us.

Two other singers were on the series of hops we would do that night: Bobby Darin and George Hamilton IV. Like us, both were promoting their first singles: Bobby's "Don't Call My Name" and George's "A Rose and a Baby Ruth." George's record as well as Frankie's "DeDe Dinah" later became huge hits.

We were whisked into a convertible in an attempt to leave one of the more riotous schools. Girls were screaming, the driver was frantically blowing the horn trying to exit the parking lot, and we were all in hysterics, enjoying the attention. Then, suddenly, the more aggressive fans discovered they could poke their hands under the car's soft top and hopefully touch Frankie, who at that time was by far the most appealing to them. That's when it got a little scary. Since Richard and I were wearing red like Frankie, they grabbed at any glimpse of red. We were all huddled in the center of the backseat, still laughing but begging our driver to make his getaway. The gigs were fun and Biondi promised to continue playing our records.

Later at a nightclub after bragging about his multitalented musical abilities, Bobby proceeded to play nearly every instrument in the band to further stress the point he was "gonna make it in this business." He elaborated on how his time was limited since he has always felt he would die young. He did succeed, and unfortunately, he did die young. Richard and I called him in New York a few months later, and he explained he couldn't see us that particular night because he had a session the following morning, one last shot with Atco Records. He was living with his sister at the time and had to yell over the voices of her children in the small apartment. "I got a thing called 'Splish Splash' and I think it's a hit!" he shouted. It was and later on we saw him at a show in New Orleans and congratulated him. He, along with Frankie and George, had many more hits in the years to come.

Cher

While I was working at Liberty Records assisting Snuff Garrett and learning the ropes of producing, one of my assignments was to hang out at the hot studios of the day and pick up on what was going on in the young Hollywood rock scene. Prior to Jan Berry's auto accident, he was often found at United or Western Studios or at the Liberty offices, working on a record project. One night we were talking in the hallway at United when Cher came bouncing up the hall. She and Sonny had come to see Don Blocker, the head of Liberty A&R, so we met. Cher, as usual, was barefoot and wearing jeans. Most of us thought of her as a groupie or hanger-on, not realizing she could actually sing. So when she jubilantly told me and Jan, "Sonny's gonna record some sides on me!" we kind of winked at each other thinking "oh sure" and politely congratulated her, never expecting her to have huge hit records for the next thirty-five years or so.

Roger Miller Meets Stephen Stills

There are so many hilarious stories and cleverly funny lines surrounding the life of Roger Miller, it would take as least an entire book to cover them. I had first met Roger when he was playing fiddle for Minnie Pearl in Rockford, Illinois. Not long after that, I saw record executives laugh at him and his songs in a downtown hotel room where Roger was bell-hopping, not really taking him or his songs seriously. Soon after Jerry Kennedy had produced the landmark sessions on Roger that resulted in his first smash hit, "Dang Me," Roger moved to California, not really expecting great success out of the recordings. He was wrong and the rest is history. He had hit after hit and would go on to star in his own network-television show, and Bobby and I were thrilled when he cut his first major version of "Little Green Apples."

One night while I was on a business trip to L.A., I got in touch with Roger, and he suggested we go to the Chateau Marmont, a hotel in Hollywood to hear "some guys" jam. When we got there we were introduced to the group, headed up by Stephen Stills, who was really riding high on the charts with Crosby, Stills, Nash & Young. "I don't know much about these guys," Roger whispered. "I don't understand what they're playin', but I like it," he added. They jammed intensely for about an hour, never pausing to say anything to us. We said our polite Southern good-byes and left. Another night in L.A., a gang of us "Texas and Tennessee transplants" were gathered at Joe Allison's house, which overlooked the blanket of lights far below that lit up Hollywood. Roger took one look at the edge of Joe's lawn and said, "Joe, you ought to mow ya' lights!"

Kris Kristofferson

Kris Kristofferson with background singers Donnie Fritts, Buzz, and Dan Penn at the Bluebird Cafe, Nashville, Tennessee

"Buzz, Buzz, wonder whu't he duzz" was the greeting I would get from Kris when we would sail through the Tuneville Music building, owned by arranger-producer Bill Justis who also recorded and wrote the instrumental "Raunchy." Flanked by either Vince Matthews, Billy Swan, or any one of his rebel clan of writer friends living and working on or near Music Row, Kris was always flashing that big and slightly evil grin as he swaggered about. He always wore his trademark black tee shirt and usually black leather pants or faded jeans. I'm sure I looked way too normal to Kris's crowd with my sport coat and slacks. I was managing Bill's publishing companies, which included Marijohn Wilkin's Buckhorn Music, for which Kris wrote. He drove an old brown Opel and sometimes slept in it next to a boarding house by Tuneville on 17th Avenue South. He often told stories about Vietnam and helicopters, sang a tune or two, drank, smoked those super strong Bull Durham cigarettes, and then went over to the night job Billy Swan helped him get, that of janitorial work at Columbia Studios on 16th.

In the fall of '98, Dan Penn, Donnie Fritts, and I sang behind Kris on "Me and Bobby McGee" at the famed Bluebird Café in Nashville. It was a fun writers' night that pianist Tim Hinkley had put together. CBS was filming Kris for a *60 Minutes* feature that night, and later at a tribute concert for Donnie in Alabama, Kris and I laughed about how we wound up on the cutting room floor. We also discussed how difficult writing a book was. Like me, he was struggling with one at the time. We reminisced about those old days at Tuneville—which later became Combine Music, the home of two of Kris's most helpful mentors, his producer, Fred Foster, and Bob Beckham, his publisher. I was visiting with Kris, Billy Swan, and the rest of his band and friends, and we had drinks at the Dugout next door to Paul Colby's Bitter End, the famed club in Greenwich Village.

Later, we all went back over to the club and prior to his set, Kris randomly asked, "Buzz, did you ever meet Bobby Dylan?"

When I answered, "No, but I'd love to," wondering why he'd asked, he turned to the smallish man to his left and drawled, "Well, this is him." Dylan had a short haircut and I hadn't recognized him. It was an honor just to shake his hand.

In '77, Kris was filming *Convoy* just north of Albuquerque and I was visiting his longtime keyboardist and my friend Donnie Fritts, sometimes affectionately known as the "Alabama Leanin' Man" because of his lovable, laid-back style. Ali MacGraw and Ernest Borgnine also starred in the movie, which was based on the song of the same title. Naturally, Donnie and I spent as much time as we could hanging out with Ali, who was sunning on the top of her trailer, and generally trying to impress her in our smooth Southern way. She was very sweet and friendly during my time there.

One afternoon, Donnie asked if I would like to meet the director of the film, Sam Peckinpah (*The Wild Bunch*, *Pat Garrett* and *Billy the Kid*, *Straw Dogs*, and others), and of course, I said "yes." Donnie took me to the bungalow where Sam was holing up, not wanting to cooperate with the daily shooting schedule. I had overheard Ernest Borgnine complaining, "That damned Peckinpah won't come out of his cabin!"

It seems Sam had a reputation of frequent participation in recreational drugs and his paranoia kicked in when he saw my clean-shaven face appear in his bungalow. He shouted, "Who is this? A straight…narc?"

I laughed as Donnie quickly jumped in with, "Naw, Sam, that's Buzz. He's from Nashville, he's alright!" We had a short visit then left. It was a fun and close-up look at this eccentric master of film direction and yet small glimpse into the fascinating and wacky world of filmmaking.

I've known many who have achieved success from our era, but Kris remains the most unaffected. He is still as warm and sincere as he was in those days when we were all paying our dues.

Buzz, Donnie Fritts, and Ali MacGraw on set of Convoy.

Sam Phillips

Buzz, Sam Phillips, and Tom Douglas Nashville, 2000

One of the most amazing, fascinating, innovative, and personable characters in the history of rock 'n roll has to be the legendary Sam Phillips, founder of Sun Records in Memphis. When I was traveling with the Jerry Lee Lewis Show in the late '50s, Jerry Lee constantly complained about Sam. But in later years, Jerry would be the first

to admit Sam was responsible for his early success. Anyone even remotely interested in the history of the rock era knows of Sam's discovering Elvis. He produced, engineered, published, and ran the record company. His original studio on Union Street in Memphis is still a world-famous landmark in the Bluff City. Not long after my recording experience at Sun, I told Sam how excited I had been to record there and what a cool session it had been. He flashed that big smile and offered a typical off-beat comeback, "What's a session?"

Jerry Reed

Jerry Reed and Buzz, watching their daughters perform in the Franklin Road Academy Marching Band, Nashville

One of the most unforgettable and gifted characters I have ever met is my friend Jerry Reed. He bounced into the tiny studio where I was working with his fellow Georgia musician, Chip Young in the mid '60s, jumped right up in my face and declared, "Son, I'm gettin' ready to tear this business up! Chet's gonna produce me!" And what a team they made.

In his book he wrote with Russ Cochran, "Me and My Guitars", Chet said, "Jerry was more innovative and put more energy into his guitar-playing than anyone I've ever heard." Jerry does this in life. Whether it's songwriting, guitar-playing, performing onstage, acting, helping those in need, or simply fishing with Bobby Bare, he's fired up! He also played golf by his own "Reed's Royal Rules and Regulations" and was "CEO" of the elite yet mythical, EGO, which stood for "Eccentric Golf Organization.Whether it was a round of golf, writing a song or sitting around the table at Nashville Golf in the Thursday morning Bible study he founded, Jerry always emitted joy, hilarity, and a loving spirit that amused as well as inspired those of us fortunate enoug to be around him.

The Oak Ridge Boys

The Oak Ridge boys -- William Golden, Duane Allen, Joe Bonsall, and Richard Sturban--with Buzz(center), backstage at a concert in 2003

I had come full circle with "The Boys," as friends and fans alike refer to the venerable quintet of gospel-turned-country vocal group. In 1976 I had written a light-hearted tribute to Emmylou Harris after seeing her perform at Hag's, a nightclub in the San Fernando Valley in L.A. with her first band, which included my pal from The Crickets, Glen D. Hardin. Ron Chancey, The Boys' producer from ABC Records, liked the song and it became the B-side of "Y'all Come Back Saloon," their first single hit on the country charts. Then, in November 2003, we had the A-side of their single release "Glory Bound," which I co-wrote with Anthony Crawford, who had recently joined the country band Blackhawk.

I arrived at the Sheraton Music City Hotel on a drizzly fall night in Nashville, where the Boys were performing at a benefit concert for Richard Sturben's, the bass singer, daughter's school. On board the group's tour bus, painted in their sponsor Blue Blocker's motif, the ever-enthusiastic lead singer, Duane Allen, was upbeat about the song's progress at the radio level and was related how important doing benefits is to the group and how he feels spiritually inspired to do as many as time allows. They have filmed numerous television specials for Feed the Children Foundation. The "Mountain Man," William Lee Golden, told me how much enjoyment he was receiving from his new-found hobby of painting while on the road as well as at home. Back in the stateroom, Joe Bonsall—tenor singer and author of several books, including the touching, G.I. Joe and Lillie—was practicing a few nice licks on the banjo, his current passion.

The Oak Ridge Boys are musically unique, great showmen, and good businessmen, having survived all these years. It has been a thrill to watch them perform and so fun to be a part of their recordings as a writer and, above all, to count The Boys among my many dear friends the music world has given me.

Where's Willie?

In 1978, Columbia Records released the highly acclaimed "Stardust " album by Willie Nelson. This lovely recording produced by Booker T. Jones, of standard songs by Willie, would reach number one in the charts and go on to sell over five million copies, becoming one of the artists' most successful endeavors.

I first met Willie in 1962 at the Liberty Records offices in Hollywood when I was working ther for Snuff Garrett. Joe Allison had produced Willie's first album,"And Then I Wrote," for the label. Fast forward to 1978 when I was back in Nashville visiting Bonnie Garner at her office in the A&R department at Columbia Records. I was telling her about my upcoming trip to Los Angeles to pitch songs from my catalogs. It so happened that Willie was playing Vegas one night that same week. "Why don't you "detour" through Vegas on your way to L.A.,?"Bonnie suggested. I said, "that sounds like fun." " I'll be there!" Willie was doing a special performance for the owners of the Golden Nugget in downtown Vegas who were having financial problems. Larry Gatlin was also on the bill.

On the way out, I visited friends in Texas and almost missed my flight to Vegas due to an unseasonable snowstorm in the Dallas-Ft. Worth area. I had been instructed by Bonnie to meet up with "Snake," who was Willie's road manager at the time. He would direct me to the transportation to the Nugget and arrange my accomodations there. "Put your bags over there," the sly looking Snake barked as I arrived at the baggage claim area. "Where's Willie?," I asked the slim man with narrow and piercing eyes that actually resembled that of a reptile. "He'll be here." was the curt reply. I would soon find myself repeating that question.

Originally built in 1946. the Golden Nugget was the largest casino in the world at the time. Long before the famed Strip was developed, downtown Vegas was where the action was. Steve Wynn bcame majority stockholder in 1973 and would later do a massive renovation of the hotel and casino. I got the idea that the show that night with Willie was some sort of a favor for Mr. Wynn, but I never knew for sure. I recall the venue itself being rather run down and in an old western style setting. The rooms were decorated similarly.

When we got to the Nugget , Snake handed me a key and said, "take your bags up to this room and wait for me to call." I didn't exactly know what was going on, but once again I did as he asked. " Am I in this room or what?," I thought in the elevator. After a few minutes in the room, as promised Snake called. ""Bring that key down." "I,ve got you in another room." When I got to the room I noticed someone else's bags on one of the beds. When I asked Snake what was going on. he told me, " Don't worry about it." Just come on down to room 304." We're going to listen to Willie's new album!" " I'll explain everything then." "Ok, Snake, and by the way where IS Willie?""He'll be here." came the stock answer.

The room was packed, the beds and chairs were filled, bodies were on the floor and in the window sills and a case of beer was brought in. Needless to say when the tape of "Stardust" started to roll on the small 1/4 inch machine, the crowded room was silent, interrupted only by occasional "oohs" and "ahs"from the guests who included several folks from Nashville and Hollywood as well. Among those in the California contingency were actors Jan-Michael Vincent and a very spaced out Dennis Hopper. I also spoke to Susanna Clark, the wife of songwriting great and friend, Guy Clark. The music was both innovative and captivating."Blue Eyes Crying In The Rain" and the title song , "Stardust," were two of the most moving and brilliant tracks on this groundbreaking recording. Everyone shouted and applauded as the last song faded away. and then the party began!

As it turned out, the bags in my room belonged to Susanna and we had a good laugh, especially when I suggested that we call and ask Guy if he would give us permission to spend the night in the same room in Las Vegas! Susanna wound up finding another room and I began to realize just how fun and crazy this weekend would be. I was waiting for the elevator to head downstairs to the showroom for sound check, when Jan-Michael strolled up with Dennis trailing him, literally bouncing off the hallway walls, giggling and mumbling incoherently. Jan-Michael was a friendly sort, so I whispered the question, "What's Dennis on?" "Aw, it's just acid man," was the reply. Later that evening, during the show, Willie would acknowledge, "my good friend, Dennis Hopper on piano," as Dennis sat next to Willie's sister Billie, banging away on the keyboard!

It was time for another "Where's Willie?," as I watched the band set up and begin the warmup for the gig. I had been chatting with Jody Payne, who sings harmony and plays acoustic guitar in the band and he assured me Willie would be there by showtime. As the strains of Mickey Raphael's harmonica bounced off the wall, I got a little nostalgic thinking how far the Red Headed Stranger had come since I met him that day in Tommy Allsup's office at Liberty Records, with his hair short and slicked back and wearing those tight fitting business suits we wore in the sixties. The sound check was brief and "Willie-less"of course. I was excited about the show as I got dressed in my best jeans and boots, anticipating a great show in a historic venue.

The band kicked off "On The Road Again" and still no Willie! I had a good spot at the edge of the stage and had a good view of the audience. After about a verse of the song, I caught the silhouette of a figure walking through the front doors and walking down the center aisle, between tables, shaking hands with the fans. It was Willie......at last! He stepped to the mic and wowed the crowd for the next two hours.

Backstage as chaotic at best. I found myself once again asking "Where's Willie?" Jody pointed to a small table in the corner. Hunkered down under the table, sitting in Indian fashion, smoking a joint, was Willie. Crawling in under the table, I shook his hand , telling him, "great show man!" Willie smiled, thanked me and asked, "You don't smoke this stuff do you? "Naw, man but I'll take a hit to toast that great album you just cut!" I almost fell over backwards as Willie laughed loudly. Believe me, you don't want to get too close to what Willie smokes! I never tried grass again.

There's a cute sequel to the "Stardust" story: Not long after the Vegas episode, I was in New York City as part of a Board of Electors for the performing rights organization, ASCAP, (American Society of Authors, Composers and Publishers. A group of writers and publishers had been selected to be present when the votes for one of the Society's elections was tallied. One of the other writer members was Mitchell Parrish, co-writer of "Stardust" with Johnny Mercer. We had ample time to chat and I took the opportunity to tell Mitch that Willie had recorded "Stardust". "Who's Willie Nelson?" Mitch asked rather sarcasticly. "He's a huge country artist, Mitch," I said, cracking up inside. "I've got to call my publisher!" He shouted at the person answering, "Give me Howie!" "Did you know Willie Nelson has cut "Stardust?" "you don't know who Willie Nelson is?" "Man he's huge in that country music!" (pause) "Well you know about it now!" Mitch barked out as he slammed the phone down.

I look forward to telling Willie that story one day.

Buzz With Martina McBride and Tom Douglas at Creative Workshop, 2002. Tom and Buzz wrote "Love's the Only House", a hit for Martina.

Buzz, Bobby Russell, and other Nashville 1968 Grammy Winners, including Johnny Cash, June Carter Cash, Steve Cropper, Mr. Otis Redding, Jeannie C. Riley, and the Happy Goodman family

Freddy Weller and Duane Eddy at Creative Workshop, 1985

Buzz with Dobie Gray at "Rockin' In Springfield", May, 2003

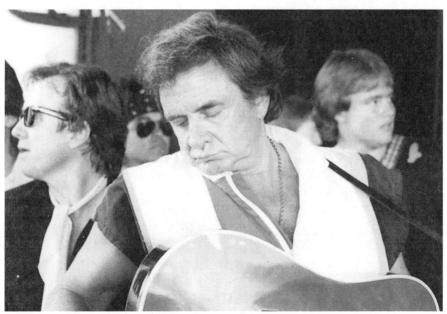

Buzz (in glasses) Johnny Cash and John Carter Cash, Nashville, 1986

Buzz with Richard Petty during the recording of "NASCAR Goes Country"

Rock 'n Roll Graffiti
First row: Mary Wilson, Frankie Ford, Carl Dobkins, Jr., Denny Lane, Troy Shondell, Joe Terry, Nedra Ross, Carl Gardner, Sandy Posey, Ketty Lester, Jewel Akens, Pat Upton, Julie Smith, Jerry Naylor, Ray Peterson, Dave Sommerville, Gene Hughes

Second row: Bucky Wilkin, Jimmy Rogers, Joanie Sommers, Dobie Stevens, Dennis Yost, Gary S. Paxton, Otis Williams, Maurice Williams, Jimmy Clanton, Scott Ross, Len Barry, Dee Dee

sharp, Joe Terry, Tommy Roe, Billy Joe Royal, Buzz Cason, Dickey Lee, Jimmy Gilmer, Dave Burgess, Jim Ed Brown, D.J. Fontana

Back row: Larry Black, Charlie Monk, Chris Negveski, Marshall Pearson, Steven Jarrell, Randy Layne, Etta Britt, Kelli Bruce, Milton Cavendar, Vikki Carrico, Terry Townsend, Chuck Schumacher, Dave "Spig" Davis

Buzz with son Taylor, in their classic 1970 Caddy

BC & The Dartz: Bob Kommersmith, Fred James, Buzz, and Jerry Carrigan

Buzz with Marijohn Wilkin, Snuff Garrett, Richard Williams, and Hugh Jarrett, rehearsing for The Statues' session

Buzz with guitar great Hank Garland, 1957

Johnny McCreery, Nashville's first rockabilly guitarist, 1957

The Casuals with Johnny and the Hurricanes, 1959

Bob Beckham

Liberty Records Promo photo, The Statues: Richard WIlliams, Hugh Jarrett, and Buzz

Harcourt Paris, Brenda Lee promo photo

Buzz performing in Midem, France, early 1990s

Clifford Curry in the 1970 Nashville Pop Festival. In the background, (from left to right) Wade Conklin, Buzz, and Mac Gayden

Buzz and Aaron Brown with '52 Ford on Ardee Avenue

Buzz and Aaron Brown with Rolls Royce in 2003

Buzz with Joe Watkins, The Casuals' sax player, and The Feetwoods, 1959

The Casuals with Sam Cooke

The Casuals with Johnny Cash at Litton High School, Nashville Tennessee, 1957

Peggy, Jimmy Buffett, and Buzz Cason, backstage at a recent concert in Nashville

The Casuals' solo act with Tony Moon (harmonica), Joey Lemon (guitar), Joe Watkins (saxophone), Billy Smith (drums), and Richard Williams (piano), 1959, Holiday House, Pittsburgh

Buzz with Bobby "Blue" Bland after ABC Records session with old friend Don Gant as producer

Alex Harvey, Dickey Lee, Freddy Weller and Buzz

*Keyboardist Mike Lawler, James Brown, and Buzz backstage at a rare appearance James
made the Grand Ole Opry*

Another shot from BC and the Dartz (Buzz's rockabilly band), 198. From left: Bob Kommer-smith, Buzz, Fred James, and Jerry Carrigan

Backstage at the W.O.R.S.T. show (Worlds Oldest Rock Starts Together), September 26, 1978. From left: Larry Henley (Newbeats), Mark Dinning (Teen Angel), Link Wray (Rumble), Buzz, Dale Hawkins (Suzie Q), Buddy Knox (Party Doll), Bobby Russell (1432 Franklin Pike Circle Hero) and Jimmy Bowen (I'm Stickin' With You)
(Special thanks to the Rockabilly Hall Of Fame)

Rockin' in England, Then Homeward Bound

I saw La Bamba at the beach now.
She likes the sand beneath her feet now.
She's number one in the California sun
When it comes to havin' fun, yeah, she's the one.

"(They Call Her) La Bamba," adapted by Buzz Cason and Jerry Allison, Recorded
by The Crickets

It all started when Jerry Allison came to my office at Liberty Records and announced, "I know who's gonna fill in for Naylor on the England tour!" He was referring to who would replace ailing lead singer, Jerry Naylor, on the upcoming thirty-day tour of British one-nighters.

"Who's that?" I mumbled, about halfway interested.

"You!" he answered, with that sly West Texas grin. I thought he was nuts and certainly not serious, but to my surprise, he was!

Jerry Allison was the distinctive, hard-hammering drummer from Lubbock, Texas, who had pounded out the unique and much-imitated floor tom roll on one of the biggest Cricket hits, "Peggy Sue." Jerry, who also sings and plays guitar, was the co-writer with Buddy Holly on several of their most successful singles, which included "That'll Be the Day," "Maybe Baby," "Oh Boy," and "Not Fade Away." These songs never seem to fade away and live on in rock infamy with bands today still performing them.

I hadn't sung with a band in quite awhile, but I did remember the Buddy Holly songs I had done in the past. I had a flashback of singing "That'll Be the Day" in Broken Bow, Oklahoma. It was the first song I had sung on the road with The Casuals during our first string of fair dates we had played in 1957. I accepted Jerry's offer, and since I had just been fired at Liberty, it came at a good time.

"When can we rehearse?" I wasted no time in asking. Knowing how unserious and fun-loving the boys were, I knew organized rehearsals weren't exactly their cup of tea. The current group of Crickets, in addition to "J.I." as Jerry was called by close associates, included Sonny Curtis, lead guitar and vocals, and Glen D. Hardin, who played keyboards and a Fender keyboard bass with his left hand, which produced quite a contrasting sound to the upright bass of original Cricket Joe B. Mauldin. Sonny lived at Sycamore Riviera Apartments, right in the heart of Hollywood, as did Dennis Wilson of The Beach Boys. The apartment complex was also the site of the

EVERLASTING LOVE • 127

murder (or suicide) of rocker Bobby Fuller, who had a huge record with "I Fought the Law and the Law Won," written by Sonny Curtis. Each time we'd get together at Sonny's the rehearsal seemed to turn into a party. So we wound up jetting away to London without ever having rehearsed our show! A brief talk-through with Sonny on the flight over would have to do. We were all more excited about being bumped to four seats on the bulkhead than we were discussing the upcoming tour. So we ordered drinks and the fun began.

This chapter is that adventure, with Beatlemania sweeping the world and bands wearing matching suits popping up everywhere. Barnstorming England in a minivan was a wild experience, and the stories from this exciting year, 1964, are among my favorite memories. I had no idea just how amusing and difficult to understand a Cockney accent was, but the first locals I encountered at Heathrow were some old blokes loading baggage. They were attempting to talk to us as we dealt with our modest welcoming contingency consisting of a handful of record company people and fan-club members. Naturally we looked a bit scruffy after flying all night and our California pompadourish hairstyles weren't as in place as we usually wore them. I took my first shiny black London taxi ride directly from the airport that morning to EMI on Abbey Road to perform for EMI, the company that distributed our Liberty product in the U.K. We had arrived in the old country with a hit record in the charts *New Musical Express (NME)* and *Record Mirror chart*. After our appearance at EMI, we were booked *Ready, Steady, Go!*, the popular rock-pop show televised live from the BBC London studios. No lip-synching, videotaping, or delays—we are talking live! On the show with us was an incredible mix of hit artists from diverse musical fields: John Lee Hooker, Dusty Springfield, The Animals, and the Swingin' Blue Jeans. The Animals introduced "The House of the Rising Sun," which I lost a bet on with Sonny, when I wrongly predicted that the song would never reach the Top 50 of the U.S. charts, much less be the number-one hit it turned out to be. It was amusing to us "clean-cut California lads" to see young Eric Burden washing his hair in the sink of the rather crude locker room–style dressing facilities we were afforded. It was their first U.K. television, as the Brits refer to TV appearances, and the song was an instant hit in England, Europe, and the rest of the world. John Lee performed "Boom, Boom, Boom, Boom," and we had the honor of having our photo taken with him for the press. The Swingin' Blue Jeans did "Hippy Hippy Shake," written by Chan Romero, a Hispanic rocker I had met in L.A., and Dusty Springfield sang "I Only Want to Be with You."

And what about us? Well, we started our song and the power went off! Here we were in a live situation with no juice! I was on the drums since J.I. sang the lead on the song, "La Bamba," which was already on the charts and we were hoping to boost its sales with a spirited rendition for the show that almost all U.K. record buyers watched. Luckily, the power came on somewhere in the first chorus, but for several measures, it was just J.I.'s vocals and my crude drumbeat.

It didn't take us long to discover that the main object of having a record out and playing gigs was not only performing, but "pulling birds," as chasing girls was called by British rockers. An unusually beautiful girl managed to make it to all of our shows near London and was friendlier to me than the other guys. I can't recall her name but it was funny when Glen D. offered to trade three of the "birds" who favored him for my one lovely friend! I refused, but he stayed on in England after the tour and she was readily available.

We were on the Isle of Man playing one show in the Casino there. We flew over from Blackpool a day early to relax and tour the island, known for its tailless Manx cats. Sonny and I rented motorbikes and had a great time zipping about the tiny island in the Irish Sea. Jerry lost all of his money on the casino tables then snuck up to our hotel room to steal what little loot the rest of us had in our jean pockets. He then proceeded to lose all of that. He had a royalty check for about four hundred dollars, which he talked someone into cashing, he bought our plane tickets back to Blackpool with the money. Flights were cheap in those days, so after buying the tickets, he and Glen D. made one last round of the gambling hall with the few pounds leftover. In 2003 we all had a laugh when Sonny Curtis told this story to a crowd of about 1,000 at an oldies event. The show was "Rockin' In Springfield" (Tennessee), "An Evening of classic Rock 'n' Roll," a benefit for Ray Peterson who was suffering from a bout with cancer. The Crickets had invited me along with ex–Paul Revere and the Raiders Keith Allison to join them on stage for "That'll Be the Day." What a flashback!

One of the highlights of the tour was our appearance at Royal Albert Hall, a very prestigious venue in England. Man, did we sound small in that huge concert hall with the tiny sound systems they used in the '60s! The main speakers in those days were not as powerful as the monitors used today, and we were all but swallowed up by the mere spaciousness of the house, where we were playing our West Texas rock. Also on the bill were Adam Faith, who was a major star in Europe, and the controversial P.J. Proby, an artist known for his wild and erratic behavior. On this particular night he made a real fool of himself by splitting his tight-fitting pants and creating a frenzy in the press the following morning. Our show went over well, but we couldn't linger at Royal Albert because we had a "double" that night, which meant we had to play another gig the same night in a different

The Crickets in London, 1964

town. I recall how we stopped at a tiny fish-and-chips place on the outskirts of London to eat the greasy fare that was wrapped in newspaper and soaked in vinegar. British fans know how to make you feel loved: screaming, rushing the stage, bringing albums and photos to the backstage, and always ready to hang out with the band until the wee hours at the clubs, where the recording groups went after their shows or on nights off. The shows were really fun and we would spend our nights off in London, taking the train back to Victoria Station every chance we got. Stan Simmons was our driver, of the scary and obviously tiny vehicle we traveled in, known as a minivan. He also doubled as road manager and was an all-around good guy. He had been with many of the rockers of the day, including Little Richard and The Rolling Stones. He told us a funny story about the flamboyant Mr. Penniman, who nightly screamed and pounded the piano to the delight of fans throughout the U.K. He was having trouble getting paid properly on a tour, so he politely went to bed and refused to get up until the money owed him was delivered. "Richard is not gettin' out of bed or playin' a note until all those pounds y'all owe him are brought up to this hotel room and put right here on his chest!" he screamed, pounding himself as the shaky promoter looked on. Needless to say he got the money.

We rolled in to Victoria Station close to midnight one warm evening in London. We had played several days straight and were much in need of some rest, so we checked in to a fairly nice hotel and planned to "crash" for a few hours. Glen D. was always ready to rock. He called us a bunch of softies as he spruced up to go out on the town. Oh how London did rock in those days! Clubs like the Speakeasy rocked on into the wee hours and a night on the town as a somewhat recognizable rock-'n-roll celebrity added to the fun. But on this particular night there would just be one Cricket sipping a lager and checking out the "dollybirds" (U.K. version of chicks) in the London nightspots.

About three a.m. we were awakened by Glen D. shouting, "You guys blew it! I've been with The Beatles! I walked in to a private room of the Speakeasy and John Lennon stood up and said, 'Glen D. Hardin!'" They proceeded to party on in that little basement club in London's Soho district, and we all regretted our failure to rave with Glen that night. The closest I got to the Fab Four was going to Piccadilly, standing in the queue in the rain to see the premiere of Hard Days Night. Sonny was with me and we marveled at the new Lennon-McCartney songs in the movie. In subsequent trips t Europe, I would have the thrill of meeting Elton John at MIDEM in France on the eve of his triumphant debut of "This Is My Song, " his first hit single, at a gala event there and in London, musician Michael Snow, who I had met in Liverpool on tour with the Crickets, introduced me to Maurice Gibb of the Bee-Gees.

The tour had been great, I'd fallen in love with England, we'd made many new friends, and being a Cricket was an East Nashville boy's dream come true. But it was time to head home. At that point in life I was wondering where home was. The free-spirited phase of my life was ending sooner than I realized, and as we winged back to L.A., I pondered my future and whether I should move on back to Nashville and start anew. California had been two solid years of good experience and training in the studio, working with some of the great musicians and singers on the Coast. In fact, Ron Hicklin was becoming increasingly busy and assured me there would be lots of studio work coming up, but I felt the best place for me and my family was back home. I can recall sitting out by the small pool behind our rented home in Van Nuys on a warm Southern California night and deciding that it was best to raise my daughter, Tammy, who was five at the time, back in Tennessee, in a safer and more secure environment. I was also anxious to meet up with Bobby Russell and get back to writing and pursuing our goal of owning our own publishing company. On the return trip home, we were towing that same little VW Bug with a shiny new Pontiac Tempest, excited about a fresh start and proving that when the time is right and if you feel led to, you certainly can go home again.

BEATBIZ in association with
VOX presents

BIG BEAT NIGHT

ROYAL ALBERT HALL
SATURDAY, 4th JULY, 196

Programme

THE CHEROKEES
THE CRICKETS
THE INFERNOS
TROY DANTE
P. J. PROBY
interval
THE PICKWICKS
BARRY ST. JOHN
THE APPLEJACKS
THE ROULETTES
ADAM FAITH

The Producer of tonight's Show—MALCOLM ROSE

In accordance with the requirements of the L.C.C. (1) The public may leave at the end of the performance by all exit and entrance doors and such doors must at that time be open. (2) All gangways, passages and staircases must be kept entirely free from chairs or obstruction. 3) The fireproof safety curtain (where applicable) must be lowered and raised once, immediately before the commencement of each performance, so as to ensure its being in proper working order. (4) No smoking shall take place on the stage except as part of the performance or entertainment.

Our Compere for Tonight

Tony Marsh

Tony Marsh is one of the most popular comperes in the country today. He was born in Southampton, and like many of today's stars, started his entertaining in the services. He won a talent contest, and on leaving the RAF started his career as compere-comedian with varying progress—sometimes up and sometimes down—but he stuck it out, waiting for the break that all show-biz folk hope for. Lately he has compered many tours by the country's leading pop stars which will stand him in good stead for his undoubtedly bright future.

Pictured with one of the stars who also appeared on Ready, Steady, Go!, The Crickets with R&B Legend John Lee Hooker, London, 1964

Hit Songs, One-Hit Wonders, and Where Do We Go from Here?

Robert Knight, Birmingham, England, 1974, performing his hit "Love on a Mountain Top" By Buzz Cason and Mac Gayden

…Where life's river flows, no one really knows,
'til someone's there to show the way to lasting love.

"Everlasting Love" by Buzz Cason and Mac Gayden

Bill Justis could barely be seen from behind the stack of papers on his desk. "Last month's mail." he said with a grin. Then looking up over his reading glasses, the man with the bald Buddha-looking head shouted, "Bills, man, bills!"

I had returned to my hometown, Nashville, to run Tuneville Music, a group of publishing companies owned by Bill. This kind and talented man from Memphis had been a part of Sam Phillips's Sun Records organization as an artist, producer, and arranger. His recording of "Raunchy" had sold a million. Bill played alto sax on the dance instrumental that teens bopped to. Former guitarist for Jerry Lee Lewis, Roland Janes, whom we had toured with, played on the record that featured heavy guitar as well as the sax. Bill was becoming increasingly in demand as a session arranger and was much in need of someone to look after his various music publishing interests. By then I had experienced the benefits of royalties from writing and was anxious to enter the publishing field.

The dream Bobby and I had for our own publishing company was still alive. Being back in Nashville would once again help make our goal attainable. Bobby had written for several companies and, like me, was ready to own part of his own music. We were closer to having our own company than we realized. I had narrowed down my job choices to Bill and my old road-mate Bob Beckham, who had offered me a writer's deal at the company he managed, Raleigh Music. I chose Tuneville mainly because I thought the possibilities of producing for Bill and learning the ropes of independent publishing and production would be most helpful to me.

I wasted little time diving into my new job, forgetting all the California fun and going about sorting out what songs were in the catalogue, all the time hoping I would find some time to write. The songwriters Bill had signed included Kris Kristofferson, who was signed to Marijohn Wilkin's Buckhorn Music. Marijohn, one of my most influential mentors, had co-written "Waterloo" for Stonewall Jackson and "Long Black Veil" for Lefty Frizell. She had introduced Richard Williams and me to the world of background singing when she joined the vocal group Hugh Jarrett had formed to do sessions and make records, as we eventually did for Liberty as The Statues. Marijohn was a former Oklahoma schoolteacher, a singer, and musician. She taught us the basics of singing and hopefully how to stay on our parts.

Since my mother had always sung alto in church, I had a natural feel for baritone and tenor, but since I did not have as good an ear as most background singers, I had to struggle more than others. One time on a Bobby Vee session Snuff was producing in Nashville, famed singer Anita Kerr giggled at me holding my hand over my ear to stay on pitch as the song faded. Her snicker can be heard on the very tail end of the song. Marijohn had always encouraged us to shake off the criticism and teasing by the "old guard" session singers, and just do our thing.

Just before he came to work there, Marijohn's son, John "Bucky" Wilkin had recorded a hit, "G.T.O.," for Amy-Mala-Bell Records, under the name Ronny & the Daytonas. Bucky formed a road band that included many of his high schoolmates, while using mainly
session players on his records. It would be rare for a band in the rock field today to use outside musicians on a session. We spent a lot more time producing rock records than the standard Music Row country fare. In any event we had great fun making records in the '60s and '70s, especially in Nashville.

The studio located in the rear of the Tuneville building was affectionately referred to as "Back 'Ere" and was a tiny monaural (mono) facility, managed by a rather neurotic engineer, Dave Manley, who had most likely been driven to his manic state by nutty songwriters like me, Bucky, and two talented and fun-loving brothers, Henry and Larry Strzlecki, plus countless other characters that graced the hallowed halls Justis owned. The studio was used primarily for our own use so the fact that we didn't even have two-track capabilities was not a factor with us.

"It's party time, boys!" Bill often declared at various times of the afternoon, and we all gathered in the big kitchen and prepared for a barbecue feast, preceded by the ceremonial passing of the Jack Daniels. Many afternoons the big, old rambling house were filled with writers and musicians looking for a place to unwind, enjoy the greasy ribs, drink, and the wacky humor Bill Justis dispensed. The Tuneville building was located on 17th Avenue South, which is now the location of Reba McEntire's vast complex, Starstruck. Our offices were housed in a stately 1920s mansion that was once an affluent South Nashville neighborhood. "Here's a six-pack of Pepsi, and a loaf of bread to soak up the fire, boys," Bill advised before handing each one of us a paper bag containing a rack of red-hot, spicy ribs from Miss Mary's, a popular barbecue establishment on Charlotte Avenue in a predominantly black neighborhood, where many of the blues artists at the time preformed. Each of us would have our own six-pack of Pepsi and bread to survive the heat and grease. Although we felt a little rough the morning after one of these "feasts," they sure were fun.

I wasted little time making friends with Bucky, who was hoping to cut another hit single to follow up "G.T.O." Amy-Mala-Bell Records, which was owned and operated by Larry Uttal in New York, had pulled a couple of singles off his Ronny & the Daytonas LP, but none had charted very high in Billboard. After sharing a few war stories or road experiences, we got down to writing songs. One surf-style ballad, "Sandy," sounded like a winner to us and Bill. As sort of an executive producer, Bill was highly supportive and helpful in making the record we had envisioned for "Sandy." We laid down the basic track in our cozy little "Back 'Ere" studio. The first generation was basically Bucky's gut-string guitar, which he plays extremely well. We added a bass, drums, and voices then transferred our original two tracks over to a four-track at Columbia Studio, where Bill arranged and conducted a beautiful string section to put the icing on the cake. After seven generations, which means that many analog transfers, our rather noisy but moody and hit-sounding single recording was finished.

"Man, that thing is noisier than one of my records," producer Shelby Singleton called to say, ribbing us a little. New York loved it and wanted it for the next single. "Sandy" was well received on pop radio and quickly became a Top 20 hit in the Billboard charts. Touring was not something Bucky really enjoyed. His dislike for the road had even led to fictitious groups that he endorsed playing shows under the Ronny & the Daytonas name, a move that would bring Bucky in some appearance money without leaving Nashville. By the time "Sandy" hit, he decided to play out occasionally. I played a few shows as a Daytona, including one on the Gulf Coast and one at the Toys for Tots benefit in Louisville, Kentucky, sponsored by the local rock station WKLO. We used various Daytonas including Bergen White on vocals, Larry Butler on keyboards, and Jerry Carrigan on drums. These three guys were at the top of their game as far as session players went and remained so for the next twenty years or more.

Meanwhile "Sandy" was moving up the charts and Bell Records chief Larry Uttal was calling for an album. At that time in music you needed to have one or more hit singles in order to merit an album release, which in the mid '60s were released on a vinyl format. We were in a rush mode to complete an album and we had a problem: Bucky was touring Europe at that time doing USO shows. There was one possible answer—cut the album in Germany. That's precisely what Bill arranged. Soon, Bill, Bergen White, and I were sitting at a bar at John F. Kennedy Airport, waiting to board a flight to Munich, where we would in one week's time, record enough songs to complete the "Sandy" album. The small table in the bar was covered with a slew of Bill's prescription bottles that remedied his various ailments at the time, which included the stress of rushing through a project with temperamental recording artists. We recorded at Willie Schmidt's Trixitone Studios in Munich, a converted theater whose floor still sloped to the wall of the building where the screen had been. Bucky and I spent every spare minute we weren't in the studio or the Hofbrau House, writing songs for the record. He had some great ones started and finishing them and working up the vocals was fun. Songs like "Nanci," "Somebody to Love Me," "Stars Shine Bright," and others on those Munich sessions were, in my opinion, among some of the most innovative and unique pop-rock recordings created by Nashville musicians and writers, and I was proud to be a part of that music. We never feared "stretching" out in our production and writing, often using chord changes, lyrics, and instrument selection that went against the grain of what was already on the radio, whether the format was country or pop.

In 2001, I was quoted in *Music Row*, Nashville's most widely read music industry trade publication, in answer to the question, "Have country's labels lost focus?" The problem is the same in the present musical era as it was back in the '60s and '70s, so I answered, "There is a need at the creative level for more diversified production techniques." Nashville suffers from too much assembly-line production, using the same players and producers on the records. As a producer, I tried and still attempt to make a record the song deserves. Fortunately, in the late '60s the doors would open in Nashville for the guys I was working with. Possibly "Music Row" record labels will heed the lesson of history and be more diversified with production in the future.

Bill Justis was about to fulfill a lifelong dream of living and working on the West Coast, arranging, producing, and conducting for records as well as film soundtracks. Bill called me in to his office, and after we had both lit up Tiparillos, our smoke of choice then, we discussed the future. "You've heard of Fred Foster, haven't you, Teen?" (Justis had nicknames for everyone; mine was "Tommy Teen.")

"Sure," I answered. "He's Orbison's producer and owns Monument, doesn't he?"

Bill nodded and told me that I needed to meet him and he was going to set it up. Bill wasted little time and I quickly found myself across the desk from Fred, who had built a highly successful independent record label mainly from the success of West Texas pop-rock great Roy Orbison. Fred produced those hits and Bill had arranged most of them, creating wonderful string lines and background vocal arrangements that are unsurpassed in music recorded in Nashville or anywhere.

"I've heard of you," Fred told me as he rose to shake my hand as we met there in what seemed like a massive office located far from Music Row in Hendersonville, just north of Nashville. I was dumbfounded since I'd done so little in the business compared to him. "Good things, I might add," he went on. I must have given him a

typical Southern "aw, shucks" grin as I tried to tell him how I admired his work and was honored to meet him. We had a good talk, focusing mainly on my and Bobby's dream of having our own publishing company and possibly a record label. I quickly discovered that Fred was seriously interested in forming a company with Bobby and me along with his partner, Jack Kirby. After a stop at Center Point Barbeque for one of its amazing minced sandwiches, I rushed on back to town to share the good news with Bobby. We had dreamed for a long time of having our own outlet for our songs, which led us to the need for a record deal.

The colorful labels of the old R&B record companies are forever etched on my mind. The great ones—like Atlantic, King, Chess, Checker, Argo, Herald, and of course, the home of rockabilly, Sun, with their distinct logos on bright backdrops— were a fun part of the new world of music, we the post-war kids were rockin' out to. Bobby and I decided on Rising Sons as the name for the new venture. Ironically, my cousin, Tim Dodson was doing artwork for Monument, Fred's parent company which would be distributing our label. The design was simple: the label name and four arrows pointing up, each arrow a pastel color, all on a shiny black backdrop. We looked forward to being the first independent producers out of Nashville to focus on rock and pop, and thanks to Fred we were on our way.

About the same time we were forming Rising Sons with Fred, we approached Larry Uttal about the possibilities of our own label to be distributed by his New York–based Amy-Mala-Bell Record Group. We decided on the name Elf. Larry was excited about adding another team of producers to his roster of labels, which already included a deal with Marshall Sehorn and Allen Toussaint, who were cutting hits with Lee Dorsey ("Workin' in the Coal Mine"), and other producers—notably, Bob Crewe, Chips Moman, and Papa Don Schroeder, who cut "I'm Your Puppet" with James & Bobby Purify. We worked out an amicable agreement and almost overnight we were in business with the New York–based company, complete with a red hotline telephone on my office desk at our offices on 17th Avenue, in the middle of Music Row. Having such immediate outlets for our productions meant we could spend most of our time in the studio producing and writing and not hassling with having to pitch our stuff to record companies.

One of the first sessions for Rising Sons was with Robert Knight, a pop–R&B singer from Franklin, Tennessee. My soul buddy and fellow songwriter Mac Gayden introduced me to Robert, who was singing with a band on weekends and working a day job at Vanderbilt University in the science lab. Mac had first heard of Robert Peebles ("Knight" being his show name) from Robert's mother who was doing housekeeping for a friend of Mac's mom. "My boy can sing so sweet," she boasted. She was right in assessing her son's talent as such, and by the time we had worked together, he had already recorded a single for Dot records as lead singer of the Paramounts, produced by the guy who had helped so many of us get on record, Noel Ball. At that time, in 1967, Mac and I and millions of others were in love with the Motown sound coming out of Detroit, especially the dramatically produced soul classics of The Four Tops and the Temptations. We were attempting to apply the Motown style of production to Robert's music. It was a bit of irony when David Ruffin, lead singer of the "Temps" did a cover version of "Everlasting Love," Robert's one big hit in the U.S. for Mac and me. That was an honor.

"Everlasting Love" came about because of a need for a B-side to what we thought was to be a smash on Robert, "The Weeper." Mac came to my house in West Nashville for a writing session and as usual brought several melodies, riffs, and grooves to work on. Two of his ideas really struck me as particularly commercial. I asked Mac, who was and is an amazing and highly regarded guitarist, to "hook them together" into one song. Mac complied and the marriage of the chord changes was magical, to put it mildly. "I can't stay to finish it though, dinner's waitin' at home. Sorry."

Since Robert's session was the next day I assured him that I'd finish it. "I'll put some kind of lyric to it," I said, with no idea of what the song would become. Neither of us was too concerned since we just knew that "The Weeper" was to be the hit of the session. In the Old Testament, in Jeremiah, the Scripture reads, "Yea, I have loved you with an everlasting love." Whether that verse was the inspiration for the song's title I can't say for sure, but I wrote the simple lyric, which soars over Mac's beautiful counter line that runs throughout the chorus. Mac loaded up the verse section of the song with another melody that was played in unison with the vocal, giving the composition yet another "hook." In fact, there is only one verse lyric in the original version, with the second verse section being an instrumental. We spent more time on "The Weeper" than any other song on the three-hour tracking session, that next day. It was a cookin' track, no doubt, but little did we know we were creating a rock classic with "Everlasting Love." The session was the first master date for Brent Maher, who would some ten years later become chief engineer for my studio, Creative Workshop. Mac, Bobby, and I loved working with Brent, mainly because he would try anything we dreamed up. We were slowing tapes down, bouncing tracks, and generally taking chances in the studio and trying things that no one else was attempting in those days of four- and eight-track recording. As for "The Weeper," for some reason it never came out on the record, maybe due to its diverse sound as compared to "Everlasting Love." Robert did a superb job of singing the song, learning it after the track date, since it was only a day old. Fred and everyone at the record company loved the record and we wasted little time getting it released to radio and the public. The record came out in the summer of '67 and took a full nine months to break in to the national charts. It literally drove Mike Shephard and the promotion guys nuts since it hit in one market, then several weeks later pop up somewhere else. It was huge in Philadelphia, selling more than 40,000 singles out of our distributor there. Mac and I did two albums with Robert, but "Everlasting Love" was his only major hit in the U.S. A group on CBS Records, Love Affair, covered us and had a number-one record in England with the song. Upon hearing Robert's album, they again covered us by recording "My Rainbow Valley," which also reached number one in the British charts.

By now, Robert was becoming a bit frustrated with what was happening in the U.K. It wasn't until 1974 that he got revenge for all the sound-alikes of his records. A little dance beat record, "Love on a Mountain Top," broke out of—believe it or not—a Nottingham, England, disco! The excited CBS promo man in that northern region contacted London CBS headquarters, excited about the action on the song, which was an album cut Mac and I had forgotten about. It was released as a single and soon Robert and I were winging off to England for a tour supporting his hit, which sold in excess of 400,000 units in England. Robert was a hit and the agency offered to guarantee him $4,000 a week to stay and work in the U.K. indefinitely. It was tempting for him. Girls were screaming and storming the stage everywhere he played, but he was homesick after just a few weeks. "Man, I'll lose my wife and job too if I stay over here, "Robert lamented. So he left stardom for what he thought was security. The sad ending to the story was that after being home awhile he lost his job at Vanderbilt and went through a divorce. He got the job back and still performs on an occasional oldies show.

Billboard magazine named "Everlasting Love" as one of only two songs to be hits in four decades of the modern rock era. In addition to Robert's '60s version, Carl Carlton had a million seller in '74, Rachel Sweet and Rex Smith a Top 20 hit in the '80s, and Gloria Estefan thrilled us with her recording of the song in the '90s. In addition we were shocked to learn of U2's random version, which was used as a B-side in '95 and on the soundtrack of the Sandra Bullock film, *Forces of Nature*. By the way, the other song hitting in four decades was "The Way You Do the Things You Do," the Motown hit written by Smokey Robinson.

Mac was building quite a reputation as a musician and his guitar was the definitive "wah wah" slide solo on J.J. Cale's "Crazy Mama," a style that has yet to be duplicated. Legendary producer Bob Johnston loved Mac's playing and used him on the "Blonde on Blonde" album by Bob Dylan. He has also recorded with the likes of Simon & Garfunkel, John Hiatt, and Linda Ronstadt. In the mid '70s, Mac formed Barefoot Jerry, which also featured one of the former Casuals, Wayne Moss. Charlie McCoy had always been a musical compadre of Mac's, and together, they played as a group with several other stellar players in the band, Area Code 615, including Norbert Putnam, bass, who later produced Jimmy Buffett; Kenny Buttery on drums; and also Barry Chance, Russ Hicks, and Bobby Thompson. The Area Code 615 and the Barefoot Jerry recordings, although not selling large numbers at a national level, are still counted as Southern rock cult classics.

In the early '70s, Mac turned his back on drugs and became a devotee of transcendental meditation. The peace and solitude from this lifestyle resulted in a laid-back and peaceful individual. Unlike the frenzy and passion his unique style of blues playing released onto the stage and recordings, Mac became a guru and mediator for struggling and stressed-out fellow musicians, many of who were battling drug problems. He would help these often gifted players to find ground zero again and start their lives clean and fresh. Mac has continued to be an inspiration to me both as a loving and caring man as well as a highly influential writer, singer, and musician.

Earlier in 1967, Clifford Curry's recording of "She Shot a Hole in My Soul," written by Mac and Chuck Neese, hit the charts. It was the first R&B record I had ever produced. Rob Galbraith was a student at University of Tennessee in Knoxville, where he also moonlighted as a deejay at a popular radio station. "Man, I got a guy you've gotta hear sing, Buzz!" Rob, shouted in a phone call in '66.

Clifford had sung in vocal groups, like The Five Pennies, and under the name "Sweet Clifford," but had never cut a serious pop–R&B record in a studio such as Nashville had to offer. His first effort was the first hit for our Elf label and quickly introduced us to the world of payola, which existed in a cash form in those days. In other words, a designated "bag man" would deliver X amount of cash to a deejay and/or deejays to buy a certain amount of airplay on a particular song. We had one first-hand experience with this method of "promotion" in Atlanta. A handful of white record company owners and producers were at the '67 National Association of Television and Radio Announcers (NATRA) convention held at the Hyatt in Atlanta. Bobby and I were there, along with Dan Penn, Rick Hall, Chips Moman, and a few others. I told Rick Hall I needed to get "Everlasting Love" and "She Shot a Hole" on a few stations to supplement the promotion New York was already doing for us. But I had another motive. As goofy as it seems, I wanted to see what it was like to pass a little cash to a radioman to get a song on his station. Rick Hall arranged a meeting at a cocktail reception to be held the evening we arrived. I was to meet Shelley Stuart from Birmingham who also claimed to be "the mouth of the South."

Diane Gayden, Mac Gayden, Frances W. Preston, Buzz Cason, Peggy Cason, Rick Riccobono,
BMI Pop Awards, Los Angeles, 1996

"Just go back outside the room and palm twenty cents, come back in, smile and shake my hand and we got a deal," Shelley advised me after Rick introduced us to each other. The "twenty cents" was a mere twenty dollars, but it was enough to get the record tested in the market with a few spins for no more than two weeks in Birmingham. If the record had "it," that magical intangible "thing" that makes a hit, then it would most likely make it the rest of the way on its own. Of course for a larger fee, one could buy some heavier airplay.

I slipped out of the room, nervously wadded up a twenty-dollar bill in my sweaty palm and reentered the party, finding Shelley and shook hands with him, sealing the deal. "I like the record man, we'll take care of you," he assured me. That was the only time I did that style of promotion! I regret that Robert and Clifford had only one significant hit each while we were together, but looking back we could be considered musical pioneers for being among the first to do pop–R&B on Music Row. The excitement and raw energy that prevailed on what is now known as Music Row during that time period is unsurpassed and never to be had again. We actually felt we were losers if we didn't have at least one or two tunes, either as writers or producers in the charts of the *Billboard Hot 100* every week. As pop and rock people we knew where the action was, and it was not on country radio, although we loved having stuff in the country charts. There were not nearly as many stations on the air and playing the Nashville country records like there are today. The pace was frantic and we spent too much time away from home, but we were breaking new ground, bringing our version of rock and pop to the world, from all places, Nashville! The silky, soulful voice of Robert and the rough, funky singing of Clifford Curry and the spirited duets of Van and Titus helped to break new ground in Nashville by recording soul music hits with none other than white producers. And for me, the dreams I used to have of being a part of the blues music I heard on that little crystal radio on Ardee Avenue had become a reality.

Jimmy Buffett, Down to Earth

Jimmy Buffett, waiting at Union Station,
Nashville, 1971

I want to go back to the islands,
Where the shrimp boats tie up to the pilings.

"Tin Cup Chalice" by Jimmy Buffett

My fifteen-year-old son, Taylor, and I were driving to his baseball game on a Saturday morning listening to Jimmy Buffett's '99 record release on his Margaritaville label, titled "Beach House on the Moon." Taylor was getting a kick out of the music as well as the clever cover shot of Buffett with Earth floating beautifully in the background. With a bit of meaningless trivia, I would add right here, I sometimes refer to Jimmy simply as "Buffett" and at times to him I simply was "Carson," Cason with an "r."

As we drove on, I proceeded to share with Taylor more information about Buffett than I am sure he was interested in hearing. "Son, you just don't know how broke Jimmy Buffett was when I met him!" I reminded him that due to Buffett's tremendous following of fans, he now grosses a tremendous amount of money on a given concert evening. I then kept quiet and spent a few minutes reminiscing as we rode to Granny White Ballpark in Brentwood. The new Buffett music was excellent and it reminded me how different things were in the beginning and how interesting it has been to watch his artistry evolve.

Charlie Monk, the self-appointed and unofficial "Mayor of Music Row," swears I signed Buffett to his first "contract" on a paper napkin at Lum's, a fast-food restaurant near the Row. The year was most likely 1969. I don't know how true that particular story is, but I do know Buffett and I had a brief but fun ride in those early days of our careers in music. He had decided he just might be able to write and sing the way he wanted and actually have people like his songs enough to buy a few. Now that part about singing like he wanted in his natural style didn't always sit well with the powers-that-be in the Nashville music business. Is that why the illustrious Dan Penn sometimes calls it "Nastyville?" I had already been involved with breaking the mold of typical singers signed to traditional record companies along Music Row. Bobby Russell and I had formed two record companies, Rising Sons and Elf, both releasing the pop and rock product we produced on new uncountry artists. We had always been renegades and, along with a few others, pioneers in independent production. We had hits on both our record labels, all the while producing acts for several major record companies. So when engineer Travis Turk mentioned he had a friend from his native Mobile, Alabama, who had become interested in a folk rock singer who he wanted me to hear I didn't shy away from listening because the singer was different. And different he was!

"If it works out with Buffett," Travis suggested, "why don't you publish his stuff and I'll produce it, maybe for your production company?" Bobby and I had been singing on sound-alike records for a company called Spar, and Travis, who was also deejaying at an area radio station, was the engineer at the studio. His friend was aspiring songwriter and insurance agent Milton Brown, who also owned a small studio in Mobile where he had the distinction of cutting the first sides on Jimmy. At Brown's encouragement, Jimmy took what proved to be an important trip to Nashville to make some demos with Travis. Upon hearing the tapes and sensing the driving and deeply creative spirit Buffett possessed, I suggested he sign a production and publishing contract with my company, known then as Russell-Cason Publications and Productions. What a character! He was amusing, charming, intelligent, and full of the kind of energy and positive outlook I still believe is necessary to succeed in entertainment or any walk of life for that matter. I've always said there are two facets of life, if you choose to do them, that definitely require a sense of humor: music and golf! Jimmy is blessed with a liberal share of it, proven by his ability to make us all laugh and have a good time. In those days, we never in our wildest dreams would have imagined the festive, party atmosphere that now happens at a Buffett concert complete with all its devoted Parrot Heads. I instantly loved this guy, a true Southern troubadour with a fresh style unlike any I had yet encountered. And although we were from different cultural and religious backgrounds—he being more educated and a Catholic, me being a graduate of the hard knocks of the road and a Baptist—we had numerous things in common, including a disdain for spiritual hypocrisy as described in Jimmy's first single, "The Christian." I felt then as I do now; he has a deep faith in God, and like many public figures, I personally feel that what we see on stage is an act and does not always reflect the private life of the person.

We quickly proceeded to record several more demos using some lesser-known musicians, some of whom later became the infamous Hang Out Gang heard on "High Cumberland Jubilee", the second album Buffett, Travis, and I did together. This first session with Jimmy under his new "deal" included "The Christian" and had among its musicians, in addition to Lanny and Rick Fiel, Bob Cook on bass and harmonica, Karl Himmell, Paul Tabet, and Travis on drums. Dave Haney was on bass and of course, Buffett on guitar and kazoo. With my love for being out on the studio floor, I joined the fun by doing some background vocals with Jimmy. I can't express enough just how important the role Travis Turk played in launching Jimmy's career. His faith and love for the music not only energized us, but by being such a talented and fast-working engineer, he managed to keep us on track. Later, I was fortunate enough to have Travis as my first chief engineer at Creative Workshop, and the Hang Out Gang became White Duck, a band I produced two albums for Russ Regan of UNI records in Los Angeles. The second record, "In Season", marked the debut of John Hiatt, the noted singer-songwriter in his first outing as an artist or part of a recording group.

Spar Studios was by no means up to industry standards, and the musicians we were working with had little, if any, experience at playing on recording sessions. So we were limited in what we could turn out as far as an actual releasable product. However, we were having fun! Making records in those days involved a lot of fun, a little work, and plenty of luck. So, we rocked on into the night at the funky sounding Spar. "Funky" sometimes can mean good, but not in the case of Spar. But with Travis at the controls, it was more than adequate for our needs. The basement studio was owned by entrepreneurs Bill Beasley and Alan Bubis, who sold their Hit-labeled 45-rpm records at convenience stores all over the U.S. Bobby and I were on salary to sing on the sound-alikes anytime we were needed. The sessions were planned to keep up with the latest hot records, and we usually did about ten songs a week. We did most of our personal projects at night and since I had not yet built Creative Workshop, having a reasonably-priced facility to work in like Spar was naturally appealing. Bill Beasley was a unique character in that he had little knowledge of music but loved to "make records," as we sometimes referred to producing in those days. Rubbing his bald head, always stuttering, and as easy to work for as anyone, the always warm and personable Bill had no problem with us singers when he would ask us to hold our checks until the company's finances were better. I doubt Buffett ever met Bill or his more businesslike partner, Alan, because we worked the night shift in the studio putting together the rather ragged demos, which launched a career that would produce years of hit records, successful books, and other ventures by the Chief Parrot Head.

Aforementioned Lanny and Rick Fiel had moved to Nashville from Lubbock, Texas, chasing their songwriting dreams, playing in clubs, doing recording sessions, and hanging out with other aspir-

ing writers and musicians. The sons of a prominent doctor, the

long-haired, hippie-looking pair were definitely not cut out of the
traditional Nashville mold. Lanny played guitar and Rick bass on some of Buffett's early recordings. These two hooked up with guitarist-singer Mario Friedel, tremendous singer Don Kloetzke, and drummer Paul Tabet, all from Fond du Lac, Wisconsin, to form the original Hang Out Gang. Buffett delighted in the humor of this bunch of renegades, related to their near-starving condition, and enjoyed jamming with them in those days when spare time still existed. Needless to say, this group of players gave us a low-budget rate on the early speculative recordings. Among the first songs were "I Can't Be Your Hero Today," "Captain America," "Richard Frost," "There's Nothin' Soft About Hard Times," "Ain't He a Genius," "Turnabout," and "The Christian," the one that slammed hypocrisy. The tracks were by no means slick and precise like the typical Nashville session players cranked out. But

one thing they had was energy, a drive and a rawness that only rock-oriented musicians can perform. The abilities of session players were more defined in the '70s in that the traditional players played most of the recording dates in town and there were very few rock players doing those studio gigs. There were, however, the Wayne Mosses and Charlie McCoys who could play just about any style. But until we secured a record deal for Mr. Buffett, we were in a low-budget situation. I'm sure some would say we wound up with a low-budget-sounding product as well! When you're having fun doing what you love with what you've got, you just rock on and live with the results.

Mike Shephard was a former Monument Records national promotional man who had worked on records by Ray Stevens, who was on the label at that time. So when Ray changed labels, it led to him being hired by Andy Williams and Alan Bernard to head up the Nashville office of their Barnaby Records, which was distributed by CBS Records. Ray had immediate success with "Everything Is Beautiful." Mike had also successfully promoted "Everlasting Love" by Robert Knight on our Monument-distributed Rising Sons Records. Convincing deejays to believe in and play a Nashville R&B–pop record was no easy task. But, this song and Robert's performance were magic and Mike worked hard for us (it's still my favorite version of the song). Once again, we had broken the Music City mold. So why not with Buffett? Just as it is with record companies today along the Row, it was very hard in that time period to make an independent production deal with an unknown artist, especially a non-country one. So I took the tapes to Mike and he loved them. "I gotta have it!" he screamed, with his brash East Coast accent bouncing off the walls of Barnaby's converted house-into-office, a building no doubt owned by one of the Row's leading landlords, Ray Stevens, a.k.a. astute businessman Harold Ray Ragsdale.

"Give us a budget and we'll cut an album for you," I suggested.

"Nah, man, I want it just like it is!" Mike insisted. I explained the cuts were just demos and we'd prefer to recut them in a more master form. He felt there was a certain magic to the songs the way they were and he would give us a "whopping" $2,500 advance!

After a brief discussion with Travis and Buffett, I agreed in what was one of my worst production mistakes of that era. Going off half-cocked because I was too eager to have a particular artist out on a record was one of many of my early career faults. Don't get me wrong, we appreciated Mike's willingness to give us a shot and we were fortunate to have someone who seemed to like the music. We had done quite well with what we had to work with, but looking back, I wish we had held out, spent more time recording, and come with a much more impressive debut record. Buffett deserved a better first shot. It was, however, a start.

Once again, enter an East Nashville connection. In a small log house on Porter Road, which he had rented with his wife, Margie—not far from Shelby Park, where I spent many fun hours as a kid—the Jimmy Buffett we have all enjoyed for all these years began to take shape. I personally feel he realized his need to become stronger playing out with just himself and his guitar. So the woodshedding began. He spent many hot, sweaty hours in the attic of that house thrashing on his acoustic guitar and working up enough songs to fill at least three or four sets if needed in the small clubs where he hoped he would soon be playing. No overnight sensation here. I paid Jimmy a salary for a newly created position at the studio, titled director of promotion, so he didn't have to take a draw against future royalties.

As he mentioned in his recent biography, he needed more income to get by so he sought out a more "real job," and with the help of Bill Williams, editor of *Billboard* magazine in Nashville, he was hired as a sort of roving reporter for the weekly music trade. I recently found a clipping from an article Jimmy had written for one of the issues. It was a club review and a bit for a local happenings column, in which he plugged a trip I had made to Texas to sign the rock group Foxx to a production contract, giving his publisher a little PR, I guess. In the meantime, Down to Earth had "escaped," an old hillbilly term for release. It was Jimmy's first album, and the cover sported the hilarious Gerry Wood photograph of Jimmy in a rusted-out '50 Chevy, partially covered by an eroding riverbank on the Cumberland River. Despite its innovative content, the record was in no man's land as far as radio, not country, not pop. His later recordings would prove his genius and knack for marketing himself. This first record was not representative of what the artist was about and Jimmy and I both knew it, but we also realized it was a start.

As for sales, Jimmy recently told a network interviewer, "My first album sold about 300 records." His CD of Songs You Know by Heart hit number one the pop catalogue sales chart in Billboard magazine—five million copies. Thankfully, my company, Let There Be Music,

published several songs on the CD of favorite Buffett songs from the last ten years or so. About three years ago I saw Jimmy at his Nashville office and as we laughed about how far he had come since those bleak early days. I assured him I had used my share of his earnings well, telling him "Man, you've paid a lot of tuition for my five kids."

We convinced Mike and Barnaby to let us do a second album. It would be sort of a concept project requiring a larger budget. So, we requested a $4,000 advance to do it. Mike got it approved, and with the additional money, we were able to use violins and violas and work with arrangements by my old friend Bergen White, who, by the way, was also a member of the Spar Studio gang. Jimmy and I had written seven of the songs on the record, some of which I thought were pretty clever and commercial for that era of music. We thought we had something. But we would never know, since Barnaby chose not to release the album. Jimmy's writing was getting better with each song, and he had and still has a gift many creative people don't possess, a strong work ethic. "In the Shelter" could have been the best piece of work on the project, and I was thrilled the night Jimmy said, "This one's for you, Buzz!" when he played Starwood in Nashville a couple of years ago. Other good ones on that collection were "Ace," "Travelin' Clean" (co-written with Lanny Fiel), "God Don't Own a Car," and the title cut, "High Cumberland Jubilee." This was the first album cut in my eight-track studio in Berry Hill, Creative Workshop, where Travis became our first chief engineer and worked tirelessly on this record. Too bad the fans didn't get to hear it until its attempted style and sound were no longer relevant. Several other gifted singers and players helped us, including Don Kloetzke on vocals, Bobby Thompson on banjo and writer-pianist Randy Goodrum, who later wrote the classics "You Needed Me" and "Bluer Than Blue." The two albums Travis and I did with Jimmy were released in '98 in their original configuration and with the art we had used on a California label, Varese Sarabande, as well as being available on Margaritaville as the "Before the Beach" CD.

"Buzzzzz." I heard a voice call to me at a Friday night football game at Franklin Road Academy in Nashville on a fall night in the early '90s. I turned around, not recognizing who the voice was and surprised to see Buffett. He hadn't called me "Carson!" His daughter, Savannah, was attending school there as did my daughter, Leah. We had a good chat, and I suggested he might be upset about the two old albums coming out in CD form, not knowing MCA had helped him in licensing the music for Margaritaville, which he owned. "Aw, no, we wanted it for the label," he assured me. When we turned back to the football game and as the teams came off for halftime, I grabbed one of my Sunday

*Travis Turk, Ginger Russell, and Jimmy Buffett with Buzz in the back, outside Creative
Workshop, site of the recording of Jimmy's second album for Barnaby*

school students, an all-star fullback, Todd Jenkins, and introduced him to Jimmy.
Todd, a quiet kid, was beat-up and bloody, but politely shook hands and managed a
slight grin. He had five touchdowns that night and a story to tell his teammates. The
next summer Jimmy would remember him at an Iguanas club date on the Gulf
Coast. Jimmy had signed the Louisiana band to his label. Todd sent a note backstage
and Jimmy arranged for him and his buddies to come in to hear him and band perform.

Back to the story, Jimmy and I were determined to secure a new record deal since
things didn't seem to be working out at Barnaby. So, on a spring morning, we
boarded the Amtrak out of historic Union Station in Nashville to New York for that
dream recording contract, the big one we needed to get his career jump-started.
Rolling through Kentucky before changing trains in Indianapolis, we broke open a
bottle of wine in between passenger cars. I recall us literally breaking the neck off the
bottle since we had no corkscrew. For us, a bottle that expensive was unusual, since
we frequently drank the screw-top wine products. We had a good time on the trip,
but not much success. Several labels turned us down, even Vanguard, the folk label
located in Greenwich Village. We also met with Paul Colby, owner of Bitter End,
who later told me, "Buzzy, I told you that kid was gonna make it one day!" Another
record company executive, Neil Bogart, president of Buddah Records, one of the

hottest rock labels then, turned us down. When I saw him in subsequent years, he'd always shout, "Man, I missed on Buffett, didn't I?"

So did all of Nashville…except for one man, considered by many as a brave soul for taking a chance on Buffett, none other than the gifted and dear friend to so many in our business, Don Gant. Several months after the New York fiasco, I received a call from Don, for whom I had sung background with a few years prior, saying "I'm gonna sign Buffett. Do you think I'm crazy?"

"Of course not!" I assured him. "Do it!" We both knew Jimmy was building a following playing the small clubs and college gigs and that just had to eventually sell a lot of records. Don was a very well-respected

producer and singer as well as being one of the best "song men" to come down the pike in a long time. He grew up in guess where?

That's right, East Nashville and attended East High, the same school all The Casuals except me attended. He cut his music industry teeth at Acuff-Rose Publications owned by Wesley Rose and Roy Acuff.

Don not only produced demos and pitched songs, but he also

produced for the in-house record label Hickory Records and sang lead on the hit pop song "Morning Girl," written by the infamous Tupper Saussy. When he signed Jimmy, he was A&R director for the Nashville office of ABC-Dunhill records. With the help of the always upbeat and energetic Dianne Petty, who would become Jimmy's publisher, Don got the L.A. office to go along with the deal even though Jimmy wasn't a country act. "Buzz, I've gotta find someone to book me," Jimmy had related to me after a day of attic woodshedding. He was ready to hit the road, and Lord knows he needed the money. I only knew one guy who might book him, Don Light, a former drummer on WSM radio's Grand Ole Opry who had formed his own booking agency to book mainly country and gospel acts. He was booking only one "folkie" he, Gove Scrivenor, a bushy-haired folk rocker. I called Don who had converted an attic office on 19th Avenue in the Music Row and suggested he listen to Jimmy to determine if he might want to book and/or manage him. Jimmy grabbed up his guitar, possibly his '70 model Yamaha acoustic. (We had both bought matching guitars from George Gruhn at his shop on Broadway. I still use mine to write with and much musical nostalgia is associated with it. I call it a "blue collar axe.") Regardless of which guitar it was, Don liked him and offered to book and manage him. Jimmy was on his way. At last, someone who could tangibly help his career and provide one essential of life: work!

Although he wasn't aware of it at the time, all the rewards and perks of living the rock-'n-roll life we all envied were in Jimmy's future. As this stage, just playing the gigs in places of some stature was the business at hand. I remember his first gig at the Bistro in Atlanta out on Peachtree Street. An old photo of the marquee reads, "Tonight: Ray Whitley," with Jimmy's name underneath. Not many were there that night, but I can confirm that at least two were in the audience, me and Tommy South, drummer and brother of writer-singer Joe South. We had fun that night, not realizing in a few short years Jimmy would headline at the more prestigious venue The Fox Theatre and draw record crowds. Atlanta would become and remain one of his strongest markets. Today, Jimmy is still one of the biggest draws in entertainment, and I continue to appreciate his talents, as well as the quarterly checks we receive at Let There Be Music, the company that publishes his older songs.

Don Gant turned out to be the perfect fit as producer for Jimmy's earlier ABC Dunhill career. He had the musical savvy and an ear for a song unparalleled in Nashville at that time. A producer does more than just direct and/or arrange a session. He is instrumental in selecting the songs, musicians, and background vocalists, as well as engineers. In the case of background or backing vocals as they are referred to, Don had a built-in "choir" consisting of himself, Bergen White, and me. The three of us had sung behind several artists and performed on jingles together. We had all worked for Alabama-native Kelso Hertson, who was very helpful and generous to me during my early session-singing career. Our trio plus various female singers had also sung for Ron Chancey on records and commercials. So the "ooh-wahs" and sing-alongs would be easy. Jimmy was always around when we over-dubbed the voices and he usually had ideas for us to try. On the first ABC album, "White Sport Coat and a Pink Crustacean", the record-buying public was granted its first look into the fascinating and fun-loving world according to Buffett. One of the songs, "I Have Found Me a Home" always reminds me of a touching letter Jimmy sent me in '71 telling me how he appreciated all I had done for him and how he was excited about the discovery of his new home, Key West.

Some of the songs may have been a little too artsy especially for the country buyers, but they were gems. "He Went to Paris," "My Lovely Lady," and one of his future classics, "Grape Fruit Juicy Fruit" continue to be Buffett favorites and of course doing the sessions for that first Gant-produced project was great fun. The infamous "Why Don't We Get Drunk?" was also on the first album, which, by the way, was done at Glaser Studio, owned by the talented vocal group The Glaser Brothers. Jimmy and I had discovered this great-sounding room while producing Tompall Glaser on "Tin Cup Chalice" for Jimmy Bowen and MGM Records. Jimmy was hesitant to do this hilarious and controversial takeoff on a traditional country song. He even listed himself as "Marvin Gardens" for the writer's credits!

Doyle Grisham was playing steel guitar for the Glasers at the time I was producing "Tin Cup Chalice" on Tompall. Jimmy and I loved his smooth, soulful style so much we double-tracked his steel, probably the first time that instrument was doubled in Nashville. It produced a soaring and ambient sound that fit the song perfectly. Doyle was a predominant part of "Come Monday," Jimmy's biggest pop ballad hit to date. Don Gant also doubled Doyle and the steel sound was a key part of the early Buffett recordings and Jimmy recently used Doyle again on "Beach House on the Moon".

Not long after the CD's release, Jimmy invited him to join him on the road. Doyle happily accepted and later told me, "I don't know how much better the road could be unless it was with somebody like the Stones!" That's the way it is in Jimmy's world now; first class, unlike the early days. Whether it was writing those rather goofy songs together, staying at the Hotel Jerome and throwing champagne glasses on the walls of Red Rock with Dan Fogelberg during Jimmy and Jane's wedding in Aspen, watching Hunter S. Thompson carry the bride over the threshold after he and I had closed the bar, or singing with Dave Loggins behind Jimmy at country music's biggest fiasco, Fan Fair, it has been a zany and adventurous trip with a fascinating man who truly chased after, caught, and made the rock-'n-roll dream his own reality.

At the 2003 CMA Awards, Jimmy accepted the award for "It's Five O'Clock Somewhere," a duet with Alan Jackson, for Vocal Event of the Year. "It looks like a rocket ship," Jimmy said. "Wow! Thank you, Jane Buffett, for putting up with me for all these years. Thank you, Alan Jackson. I'm glad I could help your struggling career. [laughter] It was about thirty-one years ago when I came to town to pursue my musical madness, and I've never won anything for anything and it's great to do it here. Thank you, Don Light, Bill Williams, and Buzz Cason!"

I received calls from all over the country about that shout-out from Jimmy. Now it's my turn. Thanks Jimmy, for the music, for the good times we had, and it's been a thrill to watch your career skyrocket to new heights!

The Whiz Kids

Bobby (center) and Buzz with unidentified (left) at
Music City News Awards

See the tree how big it's grown,
but friend it hasn't been that long it wasn't big.

"Honey" by Bobby Russell

In the time 1967, Bobby and I were starting to think we might have part of the music business figured out, at least the songwriting and publishing. In retrospect, we actually knew less about producing than we thought we did, yet we owned or co-owned two record labels. It seemed like a long period of time, but we had been pursuing our independence for a little less than five years, the time since I had moved back from the Coast. We were right at the point of fully owning our publishing; we just needed a wee bit of security. It was easier for me at the time since "Everlasting Love" had hit and I had also picked up where I had left off with my good friend, producer Kelso Herston, who was using me on jingle sessions again. Bobby did a few sessions too, but he depended mainly on a weekly draw from writing to live on. We needed an advance, salaries, or income from something other than publishing to finally go completely on our own as publishers.

There was one person we could turn to, Larry Uttal, president of Amy-Mala-Bell Records, the man who was distributing our Elf label. I was chewing at the bit to go for it on our own, while Bobby was worried about having no weekly draw. "OK, here's the deal. You ask Larry if he'll give us so much a month against our record royalties and I'll do it!" From that moment on I more or less became the spokesman for our partnership and continued that way as long as we were in business. I asked Larry and he said yes. He loved us and he loved the music we were sending him. Many times that red phone on the desk would ring and he'd come on the line with, "I love it man!" after we had sent something new up to him. We had our freedom!

The hits seemed to start immediately. After Clifford's R&B chart record, we had another minor soul hit with Van and Titus, two brothers from Knoxville, Tennessee, also recommended to us by Rob Galbraith. Mac and I wrote their first song, "Cry, Baby, Cry." The first of two albums we did for Elf was "Words, Music, Laughter and Tears", a collection of songs by Bobby. The events that preceded this project had led to instant financial success for our partnership and even more money added to Bobby's bank account or dresser drawer depending upon the size of the check. Bobby had a habit of not cashing session checks, a practice which started when a company we worked for doing sound-alike records continually struggled with the ability to pay us regularly, resulting in their requesting that we hold their checks for a few days until they had the money to cover them. Bobby had a drawer filled with these and other smaller royalty checks. At one point he joked about having several thousand dollars in that drawer! The first song in our newly formed Russell-Cason Music was "The Joker Went Wild" recorded by Brian Hyland and it was a top ten "Hot 100" hit in *Billboard*. When our first royalty check came in, we promptly cashed it, not yet even having a bank account set up. It was for $4,000 and change. We felt rich and successful, coming out of the gate with a hit right away. We were soon dubbed "the whiz kids" by columnist Red O'Donnell, who, in addition to writing an early-morning daily feature for *The Nashville Tennessean* and later *The Banner*, wrote a music business column. We would run into Red at an industry event and he'd pump us for some sort of scoop on an upcoming record release or a song which might be coming out soon.

Bobby's success as a writer of two songs in particular, "Honey" and "Little Green Apples," brought him high respect as a truly gifted writer and triggered several important changes in our lives.

"What do you think of this?" Bobby asked before playing "Honey" on his gut-string guitar from his home on Hill Road.

"Man, that's a number-one country record," I assured him, knowing that I had heard something really special.

We decided to give Glen Campbell first shot at it. He was hot at the time and we were sure he'd flip out over it. "I'll call Shane," Bobby said, referring to Bob Shane, lead singer of The Kingston Trio, whom Bobby knew through the horse business he was becoming interested in. The song never got to Campbell. As it turned out, Shane was preparing to do a solo album apart from the trio and, upon hearing "Honey," begged Bobby to let him cut it. The song was a story of a man missing his wife who had passed away, brilliantly composed by Bobby, who painted the picture in such a poignant way.

"I'll even let you and Buzz produce me on it for Decca!" Shane pleaded. After much discussion, we talked him into letting us cut him on it with the option that we could seek another version, or cover, on "Honey" after his version was released. We had little confidence in Decca, a label that had seen better years and had very few records on the charts with the exception of country artists, and we envisioned this song as being a definite crossover hit. Shane was a charming and talented man, as proven by his previous success in music. He was easy to work with and enjoyed recording with us at Foster Studio with a room full of great Nashville pickers. Shane's version of "Honey" turned out pretty well and he boldly announced to Decca that they had a two-week jump on the world. When the single came out, Decca ran a full-page ad in *Billboard*, but a few stations went on the record and we remained skeptical about the song's future. Having the right voice, the right producer, and company behind a song as important as a "Honey" means everything. It takes the complete package.

Bob Montgomery was running the Nashville office for United Artists Records. He was looking for songs for Bobby Goldsboro, who was having pop hits. The day Shane's record came out, Bobby said, "I'm going to play 'Honey' for Bob." He did and Bob loved it, so much he wanted to call a session right away to cut it. Bobby told him the deal we had with Shane and Bob assured us New York wouldn't receive the tape of Goldsboro's version until the two weeks were up. He kept his word, but when the record hit the United Artists offices in New York, they went crazy and decided to release it immediately. When Bobby Goldsboro's "Honey" hit the radio stations it was all over! The phones lit up, as they say.

Listeners were tearfully requesting the record and sales soared. Shane's record was never heard from again, but he understood and we remained friends. Meanwhile, Goldsboro's version soared to number one in country and pop. We were starting to believe what we hoped for when we had that first Jan and Dean cut: we would never have to hold down a normal job, if we could just come up with enough hit records! Not long after he had come up with "Honey," Bobby called me to come listen to another brand-new one. Once again, I was among the first to hear what would become a classic of the '60s and a future or a "standard," a term used in music for a long-lasting song—one that would be around for many years. The song was "Little Green Apples," and I was amazed that Bobby had come up with another clever and meaningful lyric almost back to back with "Honey."

Roger Miller was known to stay up for a week or two in his heyday. Not sleeping for several days was part of the "roaring" process that hillbilly musicians put their bodies through in the '50s and '60s. To roar might mean to sit around with guitars jamming, drinking coffee, and talking incessantly, or just going from one bar or beer joint laughing and partying it up. To roar sufficiently, one would most likely need help from amphetamines, which were usually available.

In any event, right after we did a simple demo on "Little Green Apples" with Bobby and guitar, Roger came to town to record. He had moved to California about the time I had. He had recorded the session that "Dang Me" was on, and then left Nashville for the Coast. We ran into each other not long after he had arrived, and he expressed doubt that he had cut a hit, even though his producer was Jerry Kennedy and the two of them had worked well together. "Me and you were smart to get out of Nashville and give it a go out here," Roger declared that evening at United Studios. I replied something like, "Well, I hope so."

Fast forward to 1968. Roger crashed at the Capitol Park Inn in downtown Nashville. By then he had recorded a string of hits and was very much in demand for personal appearances and television. But on that particular night his career was on hold, at least until someone could rouse him to listen to songs with Jerry, who had produced his recent hits. Roger wrote all of his songs, but the "someone" who would eventually awaken him believed Roger would go for "Little Green Apples." The "someone" was our friend, Doug Gilmore, who was married to our secretary, Mamie, and one of Bobby's biggest fans. At that time, he was Roger's road manager. I arrived at the hotel with the tape about three in the afternoon.

"He's been up for about two weeks, so no tellin' how long he'll sleep," Doug told me when I reached their suite. I waited several hours and no Roger. Finally, I headed home, where around midnight, Doug called to tell me, "He's up, he listened to it, he loves it, and Kennedy's trying to get a session together right now." The song was recorded around two a.m. the next morning, with the band consisting of Jerry on guitar and a bass player, resulting in a beautifully simple, yet compelling recording of the song that became a country hit for Roger and a very big pop record in England.

We lost count of the cover versions of both songs. During that time period of commercial music, artists having single hits included several of other artists' songs on their albums, which were still in the vinyl and eight-track formats. Each song had two hundred of such versions as these worldwide. One of the artists who recorded "Little Green Apples" was O.C. Smith, who was produced for Columbia Records by Jerry Fuller, who had written several songs for Ricky Nelson and was married to Annette Smerigan, my and Snuff's secretary and one of the dearest women ever to put up with and assist me in an office.

A disc jockey in Detroit played the album cut of "Little Green Apples" one morning and got such a reaction and rash of phone requests, it prompted him to call Steve Popovich, head of promotion for Columbia in New York. That one airplay by the Detroit deejay led to the release of O.C.'s record being released as a single. It turned out to be a huge hit. One newspaper quoted me as having talked to Bobby from Indianapolis, where I was racing at Raceway Park. He asked what was going on up there and I answered, "It's raining." Referring to the success of "Little Green Apples," the reporter added, "It was raining...money."

It was true that considering the business we were in and our ages, both in our late twenties, we were doing well financially. Sheet music and song folios were selling considerably more than they would in later years, and we were reaping the benefits of such sales. We had signed an exclusive print deal with Frank Hackinson of Hansen Publications of Miami. Charles Hansen liked to keep all accounts current. We seldom had a cash flow problem thanks to Hansen. Checks arrived weekly at first, then practically daily as the songs in our young catalogue were used repeatedly due to their popularity. We both had unusual ways of spending our royalties. I spent mine on my newfound hobby of sports car racing, first with a Healey "Bugeye" Sprite then on to bigger cars. Bobby splurged on a car he had longed for, a beautiful '53 Rolls Royce, which he drove around town in with a six-pack of Pabst Blue Ribbon by his side!

"Honey" won the Country Music Association's Song of the Year and "Little Green Apples" received Grammys for Song of the Year and Country Song of the Year.

Our record labels were starting to take a backseat to the publishing companies. We continued to develop artists, but we weren't producing hits on a consistent basis. We did, however, have a hit single on Bobby, a song he wrote about life in the suburbs on a typical Saturday morning called "1432 Franklin Pike Circle Hero," which he performed in his best Roger Miller voice, in a funny and loosely country-feeling track that went over well at the radio level. The song was on Bobby's "Words, Music, Laughter, and Tears", and Then I Wrote for Elf.

As you can see, we couldn't decide between the two titles so we used them both. Bobby's single hit led to various television appearances and during a trip to the Coast he decided to give California a try. It was his turn on the Coast and I was staying behind. In 1970, in the parking garage at the offices of Screen-Gems Columbia Music in Hollywood, Bobby let me know he would like to start his own company. I knew it was coming, but it saddened me in a way. We had dreamed, worked, and achieved what we had set out to do. We remained as close as brothers, but had we stayed together and combined the songs we would both have in subsequent years, we would have had quite an impressive catalogue, among the best and most diversified publishing companies, particularly of those based in Nashville. But we chose to sell Russell-Cason.

That same year we attended the Atlanta Pops Festival at the Speedway there. Janis Joplin and Big Brother and the Holding Company, Bonnie and Delaney, Booker T. and the MGs, and Chicago Transit Authority were among the artists performing. We had backstage passes allowing me to shoot some priceless 8mm film of Janis and many of the other entertainers that day. We met many interesting people, including attorney Henry Bushkin, who was Johnny Carson's lawyer. Carson often referred to him as "Bombastic Bushkin" on *The Tonight Show*. Not long after meeting him in Atlanta, Bobby and I hired Henry to sell our company. He was unable to come up with a buyer, but did get close a couple of times.

Eventually, I was contacted by the Nashville office of the Welk Music Group, who was interested in buying catalogues and wanted to talk. Bobby had previously turned down an offer in the millions that turned out to be three times what we wound up selling for. The reason: he wanted all the money in one payment. Henry represented us in the eventual sale to Welk and, with help from the commission he received from us, was able to purchase Paul Newman's home in Beverly Hills. I later visited him and his wife, who was a Nashville native and Vanderbilt graduate, in their new home. Henry had bought a new Ferrari Daytona and knowing I was a semi-professional race driver, wanted me to take it for a spin in the hills.

Another lawyer-looking guy was visiting with the Bushkins. Henry introduced us. "Take this guy with you, scare him a little," he whispered. When I returned after a speedy run with his friend who was a little nervous as we screamed through the hills, Henry pulled me off to the side, grinning as he told me, "He's a narc!"

Welk Music bought our company in 1974, bringing to a close an adventure unlike any other I have experienced. Bobby's songwriting genius and his friendship provided a way for me to break into writing and publishing. We had lived and worked like two young poets with rock-'n-roll attitudes. I couldn't have asked for a better partner and friend, but it was time go our separate ways and set out to prove that we could succeed individually, and thankfully we did.

One of the most frequently asked questions I get is, "What do you miss most about the early days? I always tell them the good times we had in as well as outside the studio and the writing sessions. Because of the off center manner of our life-styles, often things happened much differently and created funnier little incidents than the norm. Such was the case of Bobby's fourth and last wedding to his long time love, Cindy. Peggy and I had been invited as the only folks outside their families to the small private event which took place in Bobby's home on Franklin Road in Brentwood, Tennessee. Bobby's yard man was also a preacher, so he agreed to perform the ceremony. As soon as he finished the brief service, he turned to me, almost immediately and asked, " Do you have any grass?" I was rather stunned at the question but blurted out, "Naw, I dont smoke it. Sorry!" He grinned and explained , "No, I mean grass to cut!" We all had a chuckle on that one.

Two years after his untimely death in 1992, he was elected to the Nashville Song-writers Association's Hall of Fame. The organization broke tradition by letting me give the induction speech, rather than a past Hall of Famer. It was an honor to speak that night. I told how in addition to my personal loss, the world had lost a man who had given so much of himself in song, spirit, and kindness to others. It wasn't until after his death that I knew of his charitable gifts to a medical ministry in the Philippines, providing the funds for a mobile hospital. In 2000 at its annual banquet, the American Society of Composers, Authors, and Publishers (ASCAP) honored the writers and publishers of the Top 10 songs of the century in the country field. "Honey" and "Little Green Apples" were in that ten. It was a fitting tribute to Bobby and two of the greatest songs of the modern country era. I've always said a good sense of humor is a necessity in the music business, so there was laughter the evening of the Hall of Fame banquet as I shared with the audience a few of our escapades. "We were doing

in the Music Industry, the well-attended symposium devoted sessions to Buying and Selling of Copyrights, Avoiding Litigation in the Sale and Acquisition of Copyrights, International Transactions, The Organization, Free Structure and Disbursement Formulae for BMI and ASCAP and The Present

(continued f

projected on a l;
As in previous y
top stars to annc
Burt Bacharach, (
Evans, Dave Garr

The 1968 Grammy Winners

ALBUM OF THE YEAR (Awards to the Artist and A & R Producer)
    BY THE TIME I GET TO PHOENIX - Glen Campbell
        A & R Producer: Al de Lory (CAPITOL)

SONG OF THE YEAR (Songwriters' Award)
    LITTLE GREEN APPLES - Songwriter: Bobby Russell (COLUMBIA)
        (Publisher - Russell-Cason Music, Inc.)

BEST NEW ARTIST OF 1968 (Artist or Organized Group who first achieved
    national recognition during the Eligibility Year as the result of a
    recording.)
        JOSE FELICIANO (RCA)

BEST INSTRUMENTAL ARRANGEMENT (Arranger's Award for a single or album track)
    CLASSICAL GAS - Mason Williams
        Arranger: Mike Post (WARNER BROS.)

BEST ARRANGEMENT ACCOMPANYING VOCALIST(S) (Arranger's Award for a single
    or album track)
        MACARTHUR PARK - Richard Harris
            Arranger: Jim Webb (DUNHILL)

BEST ENGINEERED RECORDING (OTHER THAN CLASSICAL) (Engineer's Award)
    WICHITA LINEMAN - Glen Campbell
        Engineers: Joe Polito, Hugh Davies (CAPITOL)

BEST ALBUM COVER (Awards to the Art Director, Photographer and/or
    Graphic Artist)
        UNDERGROUND - Thelonius Monk
            Art Directors: John Berg and Richard Mantel (COLUMBIA)
            Photography: Horn/Griner Studio

BEST ALBUM NOTES (Annotator's Award)
    JOHNNY CASH AT FOLSOM PRISON
        Annotator: Johnny Cash (COLUMBIA)

BEST CONTEMPORARY-POP VOCAL PERFORMANCE, FEMALE
    DO YOU KNOW THE WAY TO SAN JOSE - Dionne Warwick (SCEPTER)

BEST CONTEMPORARY-POP VOCAL PERFORMANCE, MALE
    LIGHT MY FIRE - José Feliciano (RCA)

BEST CONTEMPORARY-POP PERFORMANCE, VOCAL DUO OR GROUP
    MRS. ROBINSON - Simon & Garfunkel (COLUMBIA)

BEST CONTEMPORARY-POP PERFORMANCE - CHORUS
    MISSION IMPOSSIBLE/NORWEGIAN WOOD - Alan Copeland Singers (ABC)

3

pretty well as publishers," I told them, "and we sure had fun spendin' that money, and in the true hillbilly tradition, yes, friends, we spent it all!"

I have observed that significant members of each generation reach a point where they might feel like my late partner when he sadly told me, "There's not a place for me anymore in this business." I've heard similar quotes from other "over fifty" entertainers or writers. I'm determined to remain positive and to continue in the wonderful world of writing as long as God wills it.

Whether performing onstage, writing songs, or producing, the challenge remains as long as the creative juices flow. We devise our own exit from our craft when we basically give up, whether it's divine inspiration combined with the desire to continue success or just the post–Depression Era work ethic. I prefer to remain in the game. I jokingly tell friends and execs, "It was tough, but fun and relatively easy breaking into the business, but now I'm struggling to break out of it."

The Birth of a Song

Dan Penn and Buzz

COUNTLESS PEOPLE I MEET ask, "How do you write a song?" Before I can attempt to reply to a question that's difficult to answer, they will add, "Do they just come to you, are you inspired, or what?" Of course, the really heartfelt lyrics and melodies almost always seem to come "out of thin air" in the form of a creative blessing. In most cases, however, today's hit songs come from regularly scheduled co-writing appointments in publishing companies or home writing rooms, bringing together two or more like-minded composers with guitars and pen in hand with lap tops and or recorders rolling, ready to go to work.

I became enamored with the written word as soon as I learned to read as a five year old in the first grade. I loved to hear *The Adventures Of Uncle Wiggly* and later on read for myself those timeless stories by Howard Garris, especially those of the old rabbitt's quest to find his fortune. Post -Depression babies who became World War ll kids like myself were often dreamers, imagining ourselves in an adventerous pursuit that pot of gold like Uncle Wiggly. With stories and rhymes of songs running through my head, I started to write down simple phrases. I even won my first grade poetry contest with this little sonnet: "There once was a bunny, he was very funny, He found an egg in a nest , so he put it in his vest!" Brilliant, huh? As I learned to read better, I acquired a taste for poetry early on, reading from a small hard cover book of classics from great poets such as Walt Whitman, Eugene Field,

Edgar Allen Poe. My father would bring home magazines and periodicals from the office every week and I soon became interested in the politics, world affairs, entertaiment and sports they contained. My favorite " light" reading was *Life In These United States* from *Readers Digest* with stories sent in by the readers. I couldn't wait to read the latest *Time* and *Life* editions to read all the latest events and the people behind them.There's lots to be said for those pre-television days after school, when we could quietly focus on quality information for the most part, that was not only entertaining but an important part of the education process. Once I started earning a little money I paid for the daily paper myself and remain a newspaper junkie to this day and pick one up no matter what city or town I'm in. I asked music row songwriter, journalist and script writer, Bob Tubert, who greatly respect, how one can prepare to be an author and he quickly replied, "read, man, read!"

Today, the business-like method of bringing songwriters together is a throwback to Tin Pan Alley and later on the Brill Building, both New York City bastions of successful creators of a vast amount of hit songs from the '30s through the '90s and beyond. These writers worked in tiny offices each publisher provided in these buildngs , mainly on a nine to five work schedule. Nashville has now perfected this proven method of birthing these three to four-minute pieces of commercial music with each co-writer striving to nurture the "baby tune" until it's ready to present to the recording world. Each new song is likened to a child we raise and put through school and then send out into the world. The writers and publishers—who, by the way, are often the same person—invest in time and money to demo the songs, as a demonstration recording is referred to. Then, the tough task of "pitching the song" begins. If you plan to co-write, find a writer who has a publisher with a strong plugger! Ultimately, the real success of a song usually goes back to that moment of conception when an idea floats into the mind of one of the writers and the team is energized by the thought that, "This could be something." "This is the one we should write today."

That's exactly what happened when Tom Douglas sat at the Yamaha Grand piano in my studio and commenced to ramble through the Spanish-feeling chords of what would become "Love's the Only House." We had started a song, with a title that neither of us can now remember and were getting nowhere with it. On a second writing session, Tom just took off on the fictional story of a grocery store checkout person waiting on a sad señorita that led to the inspirational hook of "Love's the Only House" as the singer felt sympathy and love for the señorita's life situation. We demoed the song with a slow, plodding Mexican-feel number, hoping to use it on Tom's writer-artist CD. Paul Worley, Martina McBride's producer, already loved Tom's singing and songwriting, having produced Tom's "Little Rock," a song about a recovering alcoholic, on Collin Raye. He heard "Love's the Only House" and liked it, but not until Tom and engineer-musician, Rex Schnelle recorded a more up-tempo version to be pitched, did he get excited and play it for Martina. She soon recorded it and had a number-three record and number-one video of the song which had gone through quite a metamorphosis since its early beginnings.

The spirit of creativity and love for the art of songwriting continues to both challenge and fascinate me. My primary goal as a young man was to write, produce, direct, and act on stage and in films. There were only a handful of songwriters in Nashville—now there are several in every other household! Songwriting was a natural evolution for us young rockers since there were no songs around where Garth Brooks once made an interesting statement while looking for material for a new album, that he "couldn't find any hit songs." I laughed, knowing how many monsters were lurking on the tapes and discs around town. But in my case that was true. There were few songs available to artists in the late '50s, not to mention ones that were hits! As my dream of being involved in motion pictures or the stage gave way to the excitement of live performing and recording rock 'n roll, I gravitated to creating music as my outlet of expression. Fun was an element often missing with today's songwriters. Three pieces of advice I offer aspiring tunesmiths is to have a sense of humor, listen to the veteran writers, and—the tough one—be patient.

The following is a crazy story of how another song was written: I had gone through a breakup with one of my many girlfrienduring my single years of the mid '70s to the early '80s. I called my friend Dan Penn, the legendary R&B–pop songwriter and possibly the most significant and gifted white soul singer to come out of the South during the modern rock era.

My friendship with Dan dates back to 1961, when the Casuals were passing through Alabama after a show in Columbus, Mississippi. We stopped at Rogers Truck Stop, located just across the state line. not far from Dan's hometown of Vernon, Alabama. The six of us, all hungry musicians in need of nourishmant and coffee, were seated at a table in the center of the cafe which featured the decor of the day: plastic covered chrome chairs, tables with gingham tablecoths and the ever present Seeburg or Wurlitzer Juke Box blaring away..A recent Conway Twitty song was playing and a slender young man was listening and finishing off his cheeseburger.

As he tells it, Dan took notice when our shiny, black Chevy station wagon and matching utulity trailer slid into the gravel parking lot." I saw it, and I said to myself, "that's a band!" "I could visualize that trailer filled with ender aps, drums and whatever." Dan drawled during a recent interview at the Country Music Hall Of Fame.

He got up the nerve to walk over to our table. "Buzz jumped, stuck out his hand and said, " I'm Buzz Cason, we're the Casuals, we're from Nashville and we back up Brenda Lee!" "I'm Dan Penn and I wrote "Is A Bluebird Blue," Dan fired back.

That just happened to be the song playing on the juke box when we arrived. Dan goes on to finish the story in the interview, saying that after we had left the truck stop and were driving eastward to Nashville, that I had laughed and told the band, "that fool back there thinks he wrote "Is a Bluebird Blue!" I had shared that part of the story in later years when I saw Dan at FAME studios in Florence, Alabama.

Dan later related that he used his first advance on that song from BMI to purchase a baby blue '54 Chevy, he had wanted so badly.

" Let's write," I requested of Dan, who was holed up in an attic-style office down on Music Row. "Aw man, I don't know whether I feel like it or not, but we'll do something." I told him how I had called it quits with someone I was dating and thought writing would be good therapy at the time.

He laughed and said, "C'mon, down man, we'll see."

Driving down Eighth Avenue South, it hit me: "Ya know only one thing can make you get over a woman. That's another woman!" I knew that sometime before the night was over, whether we wrote a song or not, we would be hitting the bars down on the "rock block" or Elliston Place section of Nashville and another pretty face might take my mind off the latest girlfriend.

"Yeah, we can write that," Dan said when he heard the one line I had going. "But first, let's go have a beer."

"Oh no," I stopped him, knowing if we left that office and realizing it was the happy hour time of the evening, we'd never get back to the song. "Let's finish it now, it's just a little country thing," I urged him. Dan is always great with melodies, lyrics, and grooves having already co-written "Cry Like A Baby," "Sweet Inspiration," I'm Your Puppet," and "The Dark End of the Street." His co-writers included the legendary Spooner Oldham and noted producer-guitarist Chips Moman.

I blocked the doors several times when Dan would get restless and tried to leave. In most cases, it takes two or more sessions to finish a song, but that night on Music Row, two basically R&B men turned out a complete country song, "Another Woman," recorded by T.G. Shephard, who had a Top 10 hit with it. It was also later released as a single by Billy "Crash" Craddock without much success. It turned out to be a good two-hour project for us. My roving eye during my single days also gave Dan and me another zany and repulsively titled country rocker, "They're All Too Ugly Tonight," an irreverent 6/8 time song which was recorded by my rockin' old friend, Jerry Lee Lewis and released on Mercury Records and produced by another great friend, Jerry Kennedy a legendary producer and guitarist. The fact that I had first heard Jerry Lee's Sun Records on my crystal radio back on Ardee Avenue in East Nashville and the fact we had traveled with him in the early rock-'n-roll days made this record more special.

Dan and I had been down on Nashville's "Rock Block" at T.G.I. Fridays and were joking that there were no attractive ladies (there must have been one or two at least) in the crowded, popular bar area. "Yeah, they all too ugly tonight," Dan quipped. Thus, another song very few people ever heard was started!

Nowadays, in the more civilized stage of my life, we usually write during normal business hours, starting around 10:00 and winding up at 3:00 or 4:00 in the afternoon. If my co-writers and I reach a verse and a chorus, it qualifies us to go to lunch

—otherwise we are required to overdose on coffee and keep going until something decent comes together. We always do a "work tape" after nailing down the melody and almost perfect lyrics. Works tapes are essential to capturing the original concept of a song. I was recently writing with Steve Wariner, who besides having a beautiful voice and having sold millions of records as an artist, was an accomplished writer and unbelievable guitarist. On top of all of this, he had a state-of-the-art studio on his farm just outside of Nashville. We wrote what I felt one day would be a hit song for someone and it was time to do a work tape. We both laughed as we attempted to record the work tape verse on a static-filled "ghetto blaster" Steve had sitting in the corner of his control room with all of its sophisticated gear. The idea is to get it down on tape on anything, as long as you can later decipher what it is, so it can be taken to the next level. It's a process that works and somehow continues to be exciting and fresh every time you sit down to start a song. Of course you have bad days when nothing comes out, but the winners outweigh the multitude of losers. "A hit cures lots of ills," I heard an old writer advise in my early career. He was right: the healing begins when that first royalty check comes in, or better yet, the special moment when you hear it on the radio for the first time. I always keep in mind when and where the song I am hearing was born—and I smile.

The Casuals with Brenda Lee at the Holiday House, Pittsburg, Pennsylvania, 1959

Songwriter Gallery

Roy Acuff

From left: Buzz, Roy Acuff, Eddy Lee and Oswald, backstage at the Grand Ole Opry. Roy Acuff, the great country legend always had an "open door" policy for his dressing room at the Opry. This particular evening, my friend, Eddy Lee from New Mexico and I stopped in to see Mr. Acuff and snapped this priceless photo with him and his long time sidekick, Brother Oswald.

Bill Monroe

Bill Monroe, writer of "Blue Moon Of Kentucky," and Buzz, backstage with the founding father of Bluegrass music, Bill Monroe, a member of the Rock 'n Roll, Country and Blue Grass Halls Of Fame.

John D. Loudermilk

Pictured at the Country Music Hall Of Fame are Buzz and John D. Loudermilk, Hall Of Fame Songwriter of "Waterloo", "then You Can Tell Me Goodbye", "Abilene", "Break My Mind" and countless other hits. My band played on several of John D's early demo recordings.

Dan Penn

Buzz with Dan Penn, at the "Poets and Prophets" presentation at the Country Music Hall of Fame. Dan is co-writer of rock and R&B classics such as "Do Right Woman", "Cry Like A Baby", "I'm Your Puppett", "It Tears Me Up", and also co-wrote "Another Woman" with me, which was a hit for TG Shepard.

Oak Ridge Boys

Left to Right With Oak Ridge Boys: Joe Bonsell, Duane Allen, Buzz, Richard Sturban, and Bill Golden in Cannes, France for the MIDEM conference in 1979.

Neil Young

Buzz with rock legend, Neil Young at the Nashville preview party and tribute to the musicians who played and toured as Neil's International Harvester Band. The event also celebrated the release of Neil's "A Treasure" album. Neil and I discussed everything from our mutual love for "Detroit Iron" referring to classic American cars, to my days with Brenda Lee. He asked if I was still "out there playing music," and I said I was and we talked about my early days with Brenda Lee, who he greatly admires.

Everlasting Love

THERE'S A GREAT DIFFERENCE in the love affair I have had with music since I first heard my mother sing to me and the melodies and lyrics that have followed, and the love so everlasting which was promised and is being fulfilled by my heavenly father. The same goes for the precious ones I love and receive love from in this life. As much as they all mean to me, at days end I turn to Him for that assurance and enduring grace He offers. We are sustained by His mercy and He places those special ones in our paths as a divine way to show just how much He truly cares for us.

There's a certain continuing beauty to the music we love, no matter how melodic or even how raw it may be. I always disagree with fellow veterans of the business when they say "everything on the radio" is terrible, when that's not always the truth. Music as with any of the arts changes with the times. In the case of the rock 'n roll culture and the way it has evolved, I find much of it contrived and too vulgar to stomach. But not all of it. And when it comes to the older classic songs and even some of those in today's marketplace, we never seem to tire of hearing them and singing along, whether it be from a radio or television performance or a tune we've saved on our ipod. If the song has a catchy "hooky" chorus, we're all in. This sustainability of a composition has been the case of mine and Mac's most popular song. I often refer to it as "doing a medley of my hit," prior to playing "Everlasting Love" in a live setting. Without Mac's sheer musical genius and deep soulful roots, the song would have never happened. We did and still do make a good team and I'm sure thankful and blessed for that.

Following Robert Knight's landmark recording, which is still my favorite version by the way, came multiple covers of the song. Interestingly, when I play the song live, many folks will ask, "Now who all has recorded that?" They seem to know the song but not always the artist. I usually rattle off a few of the singers and the year that each major version was a hit and it all comes back to them and they recall how old they were and what they were doing in life in a particular year when the song happened to be a hit on the airwaves.   In 2009, Jody Williams , vice president at BMI (Broadast Music Inc.) presented Mac and me with citations commemorating seven million spins for "Everlasting Love" and a special award to Robert Knight, who was at Puckett's Grocery in Franklin, Tennessee, that night to sing his great version of the song for an enthusiastic crowd , who gave him a standing ovation.

My recollection of a singer who first caught my attention is in the person of Hank Williams, who dominated the radio and the juke boxes in the late forties and early fifties. He sounded like an older, seasoned singer , although he was just in his twenties when he had his unbelievable string of hits. When I wrote and recorded "Hats Off To Hank" for my friend Chris Thomas' Palo Duro Records, I mentioned in the liner notes that Hank was "country, rockabilly, rhythm and blues" all rolled into one package and I added , "thank you man." He left us when he was only twenty nine. What an incredible body of work for such a short period of time.

Hank epitomizes the sustainability of real songs and the magical recordings he and the other artists who have painted my musical landscape over the years. From all the rhythm and blues pioneers of Atlantic Records to the innovaters of Motown and Stax on through Bob Dylan, whose seemingly endless supply of creations continues to amaze us, I remain in awe. I still get chills when I hear a Brenda Lee record. The energy of John Fogarty in always fresh and Tom Petty, who I saw with the Heartbreakers in 2010, cuts through like he did when he first arrived. There are so many artists I'm drawn to like the diverse Shawn Mullins, the raw veteran Ray Wylie Hubbard, as well as Kentucky's Chris Knight. I could go on and on, because you see with me it is a lasting affair I have with this art form we all love so. To say I've been blessed by the opportunity to hear, to sing and to know some of those who make the music is an understatement.

One thing all these performers have in common: they love what they do and they love the thrill of playing live, either to a sold out, large venue, a small music festival or a bar. The energy that goes back and forth from the stage to the audience and vice versa is hard to explain. The travelling, the being away from home and all the other difficulties of the road seem to disappear when you hit that first chord. If I may, and at the sake of being corny, I'll term those emotions as an "everlasting" feeling you don't forget.

Actor Kevin Costner and his band , Modern West occasionally rehearse in my studio. Here's a guy who has achieved and is still achieving much in films, but he's travelling the world playing music. Why? Because he loves it. That's what I'm talking about!

ENCORE

I OFTEN WONDER WHAT path my life would have taken had I heeded Minnie Pearl's advice that night in Broken Bow, Oklahoma. I doubt I would have wound up in music, and I probably would have missed the fun and adventure I continue to experience in the wacky world of this business. I would have liked to have that college degree my mother wanted so badly for me. It's hard to get away without one nowadays and have much success. That was another century and the standards are different regarding higher education today.

To me, the rock-'n-roll dream had less to do with the music and more to do with desire to experience the freedom and excitement only a world of such rhythmic adventure the music could provide. But after a brief stint in the spotlight and long after the sounds of girls screaming had died out, I realized it is the music that drives us and fulfills the dream. There's still no thrill like hearing one of my new songs on the air for the first time. It's that radio thing, the medium that seems to make the song larger than life, like one might feel seeing a finished film on the screen for the first time.

We set out as first as fun-seekers, with no great aspirations other than just going out and putting on a good show. The band and I just wanted work. We were playing music for a living. If somehow fame and fortune came as a result of our efforts, then we'd take it. Not until I got in the song part of the music business, did I get serious about presenting a fresh and polished product and after meeting Bobby Russell, I felt the pressure to succeed, realizing that the standard of writing had been raised. Bobby was way ahead of me in putting songs together and I was learning from him every step of the way.

In the late '50s, there was a handful, maybe no more than a dozen or so, of us young rock-'n-roll and rockabilly singers and writers on the streets of Nashville, where there few doors at all to hear us, much less any open ones. The group included a young Illinois girl, who was the closest thing to a female Elvis I had ever seen. She had the moves, the voice, and a mother who was more than just a typical stage mom, a positive motivator, filled with enthusiasm for not only her daughter, but for us, the band, that backed her on several dates. The girl was Jackie Dee, who later moved to California and became Jackie DeShannon and recorded for Liberty with hits including, "What the World Needs Is Love," "Needles and Pins," and "When You Walk in the Room." Like Bobby Darin, she had tremendous desire to make it in music, relentlessly pursuing her craft. Because her style was a little "out of the box," Jackie was a perfect example of an artist Nashville didn't understand. She had the talent, the drive, and the energy, and above all, she had "the dream."

Life was reckless in those "pioneer days " on the road. When I think about the close calls we had on the highway, I shudder to think of the disasters that could have happened. The entertainers now have planes, luxury buses, and most of the comforts of home, and although it's still hard, it can't compare to stuffing six guys in a station wagon and heading out for a jump of eight or nine hundred miles.

I still wouldn't have traded my life during that time period for anything else. The interesting characters and just plain old good people made it a fun and exciting trip to be on. In the field of entertainment, where you hear so much trash, there were many wonderful people who had a positive influence on me in my personal life as well as in this zany up-and-down career I've been experiencing. From these individuals I've learned that to survive it in any walk of life it takes dedication, preparation, determination and an ever present sense of humor!

In some ways I'm glad I didn't take Minnie Pearl's advice that night when she told me that first night in Broken Bow to "get yourself back to Nashville and get yourself in school" referring to the fact that I had turned down a small art scholarship to Peabody College, thus disappointing my mother in particular. She had not only worked her way through college, but also a boarding high school in Lynn, Alabama. She graduated from Tennessee College for Teachers in 1929! My daughter Kristy graduated from the same school, which is now Middle Tennessee State University sixty years later! Kristy's graduation as well as the other college degrees either received or being finished by my other children would have thrilled my mother as well as well my father. Leah garduated from the University of Georgia, Parker from Belmont University, with Tammy at the University of Phoenix and Taylor at Middle Tennssee State University.

There has always been a serious void in my life that only a college education could have filled. But I had hit the road at seventeen, never looking back, not advisable to the youth of today. (Do you hear that, kids?) What a different world I grew up in!

The early days of rock 'n roll were a result of white singers and musicians attempting to play rhythm and blues. We couldn't help but mix the musical roots of our culture in with this intoxicating, sensual and danceable groove of music we had fallen in love with. All the perks of stardom and fame were not our goals. We just wanted to perform. At a recent oldies show at the Ryman Auditorium in Nashville, Bruce Channel of "Hey Baby" fame agreed. "Hell, we just want someplace to play," he said.

Girls had always screamed for rock-'n-rollers. That was one perk we did get a kick out of. As we traveled all over the country backing the stars, we were fascinated by the enthusiastic fans and how they sometimes pursued the singers and musicians. There was very little drinking in our group and almost no drug use. We did have fun, but there was an element of innocence that I'm afraid doesn't exist these days.

It was the night of the ultimate encore. We were appearing with Brenda at the Concord Hotel in Kiamesha Lake, in Upstate New York in an area known as the

Borscht Belt, where wealthy Jewish people go for weekend getaways and vacations. Brenda was sharing the bill with comic great, Jackie Mason. It was a hoot to see six Southern boys lapping up the lavish lifestyle of this beautiful resort. We just couldn't believe the five course breakfasts, sumptuous lunches, and dinners they served. On this particular gig, we were entitled to eat free, so six starving musicians dug in!

The audience was great that night. In lieu of applause, each person was given a small wooden mallet to bang on the table at the end of a song or a joke they liked. Brenda was "on" that night as always but maybe with a little extra edge that night. Dub Allbritten had had a sly grin on his face as we came off the stage after the thunderous sound of the rapping after Brenda's last song. "Let's let it run tonight!" he said. This meant instead of returning to the stage for one more song, Brenda would sing on as long as they were going as wild as they were. "Always leave them wanting more," is the old showbiz saying. "What would be enough tonight?" we wondered. Ten songs later they were still rapping their mallets! So on that special night in the Catskills, for one show only, Brenda Lee and The Casuals practically repeated their entire show and still had them on their feet wanting more. What an entertainer she was that night! It truly was the night of the ultimate encore.

God has generously blessed this undeserving East Nashville boy and allowed me to work in a creative environment I still love. They say timing is everything and I sure came along during an awesome era. The joy of the journey has confirmed so many times how blessed I am and how much I love what I do. I continue to enjoy the work: writing, producing, occasionally performing and like the fans, (I'm one myself) I still keep coming back for more.

On a warm sunny day in Berry Hill, Tennessee, the azaleas were starting to bloom, the birds were singing, and I looked out my window at the gravel driveway of the studio where I'd worked and played for thirty years. A thin, pale man with short hair stands in front of a Saab convertible, eyes closed, facing west, soaking up the rays, with a peaceful smile on his face. I walked out to get something out of the car and I recognize him as Levon Helm. Yes, the Levon from The Band, drummer and singer of "Up on Cripple Creek," "The Night They Drove Old Dixie Down," and numerous other classics recorded in Upstate New York in the '70s.

"I brought my drums down from Woodstock. I love to drive," he told me. He was recording in the studio next door. "I was hoping the weather would be like this," he said with a smile. Although we had never met before, we talked as if we were old friends, speaking the language of music, reminiscing about mutual acquaintances, his blue-gray eyes lighting up when the name of Earl Palmer, the legendary New Orleans drummer was mentioned.

It is 2011, yet still I keep meeting warm, soulful, and gifted people like Levon. The music flows on. There's bound to be a song blowing in on that balmy Southern breeze and I just might have to reach up and grab it.

Buzz Cason Songwriter Discography

- 1957   My Love Song for You (Cason-Williams), The Casuals, DOT
- 1959   Tennessee (Cason-Russell), Jan and Dean, LIBERTY
- 1962   Popsicle (Cason-Russell), Jan and Dean, LIBERTY
- 1962   Soldier of Love (Cason-Moon), Arthur Alexander, DOT
- 1964   The Waiting Game (Cason), Brenda Lee, DECCA
- 1966   Sandy (Cason-Wilkin), Ronny and the Daytonas, AMY/MALA
- 1967   Everlasting Love (Cason-Gayden), Robert Knight, RISING SONS
- 1967   Cry Baby, Cry (Cason-Gayden), Van and Titus, ELF
- 1968   Everlasting Love (Cason-Gayden) (#1 in UK), The Love Affair, CBS
- 1968   My Rainbow Valley (#1 in UK), The Love Affair, CBS
- 1972   Ann, Don't Go Running (Cason), Tommy Overstreet, DOT
- 1974   Love On A Mountain Top (Cason-Gayden), Robert Knight (Top Ten UK), MONUMENT
- 1974   Everlasting Love (Cason-Gayden), Carl Carlton, BACKBEAT
- 1976   Another Woman (Cason-Penn), T.G. Shephard, MOTOWN
- 1979   A Million Old Goodbyes (Cason-Russell-Gibb), Mel Tillis, WARNER BROS.
- 1982   Everlasting Love (Cason-Gayden), Rachel Sweet and Rex Smith, CBS
- 1982   Bar Wars (Cason), Freddy Weller, COLUMBIA
- 1985   Timeless and True Love (Cason-Black-Roberts), The McCarter Sisters, WARNER BROS.
- 1985   Soldier of Love (Cason-Moon), Marshall Crenshaw, WARNER BROS.
- 1990   Soldier of Love (Cason-Moon), The Beatles, CAPITOL
- 1995   Everlasting Love (Cason-Gayden), U2, ISLAND
- 1998   Everlasting Love (Cason-Gayden), Gloria Estefan, SONY
- 1999   Soldier of Love (Cason-Moon), Pearl Jam, SONY

- 2000   Love's The Only House (Cason-Douglas), Martina McBride, RCA

- 2001   The Bird Song (Cason-Thrasher), Meredith Edwards, MERCURY

- 2002   Radio Cafe CD (Crawford-Cason), Anthony Crawford, ARENA

- 2003   Timeless and True Love (Cason-Roberts-Black), Jeannie Kendall and Alan Jackson, ROUNDER

- 2003   Glory Bound (Cason-Crawford), Oak Ridge Boys, SPRING HILL

- 2004   The Bird Song (Cason-Thrasher) Malibu Storm ROUNDER

- 2005   Everlasting Love (Cason-Gayden) Jamie Cullum UNIVERSAL UK Soundtrack, Bridget Jones, The Edge Of Reason

- 2006   Soldiers Of Love The Derailers PALO DURO title cut, Soldier Of Love (Cason-Moon) plus six others songs co-written with Brian Hofeldt

- 2007   Hats Off To Hank CD Buzz Cason PALO DURO

- 2008   Guaranteed To Satisfy The Derailers PALO DURO Three songs co-written with Brian Hofeldt

- 2009   Busload Of Love CD Buzz Cason PALO DURO

- 2010   Working Without A Net CD Buzz Cason ArenA

Other songs recorded by Jimmy Buffett, The Crickets, Freddy Cannon, Gary Lewis and the Playboys, Placido Domingo, Jerry Lee Lewis, Gary Allen, Gene Watson, Jerry Reed, Dolly Parton, Bobby Vee ,Rick Nelson, and believe it or not, Rudy Valee.

CAREER HIGHLIGHTS

1956   Forms Nashville's first rock-'n-roll band, The Casuals, with fellow East Nashvillians Richard Williams, Billy Smith, Chester Power, and Johnny McCreery.

First performance with band, March 16, 1956, at Lebanon High School, Lebanon, Tennessee, hometown of his father, Roy Cason.

1957   Writes first song, "My Love Song for You," recorded by The Casuals, produced by Nashville disc jockey Noel Ball for Nu-Sound Records, and later released on Randy Wood's Dot Records, also in 1957.

Appears regularly on Noel Ball's popular Nashville television show Saturday Showcase with The Casuals. Band is in high demand for personal appearances in Middle Tennessee area. Meets Elvis Presley in Memphis at WHBQ Radio, while promoting record there.

Upon graduation from Litton High School in suburban Inglewood, on the outskirts of Nashville, goes on first tour with The Casuals, opening for and backing acts on a Grand Ole Opry show that featured various stars, including Minnie Pearl, Mel Tillis, Kitty Wells, and other country acts. Performs rockabilly and rock as a novelty to help draw younger fans to the venues that consisted mainly of county fair dates throughout the Midwest. At seventeen, works as a full-time performer.

1958   Meets fellow Nashvillian and hopeful songwriter Bobby Russell, and they collaborate on their first song, "Tennessee," which is released under the group name The Todds and becomes their first chart record when Jan and Dean release their version of the song on Liberty Records. Opens shows for Jerry Lee Lewis, Eddy Cochran, and Carl Perkins.

1959   Signs first recording contract with Liberty Records as part of The Statues, a vocal group formed by Hugh Jarrett, former bass singer of the Jordanaires. First single, "Blue Velvet," hits Billboard Hot 100 charts. Hollywood record producer Snuff Garrett produces their records.

Records first solo recording, "Look For A Star," under the name "Garry Miles," also for Liberty. Song makes Billboard's Top 20 charts. Continues to tour with Brenda Lee, performing as Garry Miles, and as part of The Casuals, backs Brenda and other top acts, including Fabian, Johnny and Dorsey Burnette, Chubby Checker, and others.

1962   Resigns as singer for The Casuals and accepts job as Snuff Garrett's assistant and as producer for Liberty Records in Hollywood, produces records on The Crickets and Buddy Knox. In England, The Beatles perform a live version for radio of "Soldier of Love," co-written with fellow Casual Tony Moon. Song will later be released as part of Live at the BBC on Capitol. The writers are not aware of The Beatles cover until bootleg version surfaces in 1980.

1964   Job at Liberty is terminated. Joins Crickets and tours England at height of Beatlemania. Production of "La Bamba" by The Crickets hits charts in England. Moves back to Nashville.

1966   Co-writes hit single "Sandy" with Bucky Wilkin for the group Ronny & the Daytonas.
Forms Rising Sons Music and Records with Bobby Russell and Fred Foster of Monument Records fame. Also forms Elf with Bobby and Larry Uttal of Amy-Mala-Bell Records of New York.
Co-writes "Everlasting Love" with Mac Gayden. Co-produces Robert Knight's "Everlasting Love" with Mac.
Becomes partner with Bobby Russell in Russell-Cason Music. Company's first song, "The Joker Went Wild," written by Bobby and recorded by Brian Hyland becomes pop hit. "Honey" and "Little Green Apples," both also written by Bobby, become major multimarket hits.

1969   Produces "1432 Franklin Pike Circle Hero" with Bobby as artist for Elf Records. Company moves to Berry Hill, in South Nashville, becoming first commercial office in the area.

1970   Buzz and Bobby decide to form separate publishing companies and sell Russell-Cason Music.
Recording engineer Travis Turk introduces Buzz to Jimmy Buffett. Travis and Buzz produce Jimmy's first album, Down to Earth, for Barnaby Records. Buzz builds Creative Workshop, first multitrack recording studio in Berry Hill, later called "Studio Row." Numerous artists including Leon Russell and Jimmy Buffett record in Creative Workshop. Jimmy's High Cumberland Jubilee is produced by Travis, containing songs co-written by Jimmy and Buzz.

1974   Russell-Cason is sold to the Welk Music Group. Carl Carlton records "Everlasting Love" at Creative Workshop, produced by "Papa" Don Schroeder for Backbeat records, where it becomes a million-record seller. Buzz accompanies Robert Knight to England where Robert's record of "Love on the Mountain Top" was a Top 10 hit on CBS Records.

1976   Brent Maher becomes chief engineer of Creative Workshop. Tom Hidley of Westlake Audio redesigns the studio, bringing it up to a state-of-the-art facility. It becomes home to The Gatlin Brothers, who proceed to record best-selling albums under the supervision of producer Fred Foster. The Doobie Brothers also recorded a portion of their Stampede album. Olivia Newton-John record her highly acclaimed 1976 album, Don't Stop Believin', for MCA in Creative Workshop.

1979   Steve Gibb's "She Believes in Me" is a number-one record for Kenny Rogers, produced by Larry Butler for United Artists Records, becoming biggest selling song in Buzz's publishing career.

Song receives Grammy nomination for Song of the Year.

Is elected to Nashville Board of Governors of NARAS and as a National Trustee.

Travels to Melbourne, Australia, where he produces country group Bluestone for Image Records. Learns of Beatles' recording of "Soldier of Love" from bootleg tapes of 1962 BBC radio show.

1981   Builds Creative Workshop II. Brent produces initial hits on The Judds in the new studio. Rodney Crowell, Roy Orbison, and Emmylou Harris are among the clients of the new facility. Brent, Dan Williams, and Tom Smith purchases the studio, renaming it Creative Recording. In 2002, it is sold to John McBride and is where projects on his wife, Martina, are produced, as well as sessions with the likes of Kid Rock as a producer, Sheryl Crow, John Hiatt, and The Red Hot Chili Peppers take place. Today, the studio is known as Blackbird Recording.

1982   Continues to write, publish, and produce. Catalogue hits include "I'll Come Back as Another Woman," recorded by Tanya Tucker, written by Richard E. Carpenter and Kent Robbins; "Another Woman," recorded by T.G. Shephard, written by Buzz and Dan Penn; "Timeless and True Love," recorded by the McCarter Sisters, written by Buzz, Austin Roberts, and Charlie Black; "I Broke It, I'll Fix It," recorded by River Road, written by Buzz and Byron Hill; "Love's the Only House," recorded by Martina McBride, written by Buzz and Tom Douglas; and in 2001, "The Bird Song" recorded by Meredith Edwards and written by Buzz and Neil Thrasher.

In 2000 Buzz appears on Rock 'n Roll Graffiti, a video special produced by Larry Black for home video sales and Public Television. The reunion of classic rock performers includes Tommy Roe, Billy Joe Royal, Dickey Lee, Gary Paxton, Carl Gardner of the Coasters, Mary Wilson of the Supremes, Dee Dee Sharp, Bucky Wilkin of Ronny & the Daytonas, Otis Williams of The Charms, Maurice Williams of The Zodiacs, Len Barry, Frankie Ford, Carl Dobbins Jr., D.J. Fontana, the Browns, Dave Burgess of the Champs, Jewel Aiken, Kitty Lester, Sandy Posey, and co-host Gene Hughes.

2002   Co-produces Radio Cafe with artist Anthony Crawford. Continues to write and perform at classic rock-'n-roll shows and writers' nights.

2003   Co-produces second CD on Anthony Crawford. Writes "Glory Bound" with Anthony Crawford, recorded by the Oak Ridge Boys and released on their Colors CD, which was nominated for a Grammy by NARAS members. Is named to Legislative Committee of NSAI (Nashville Songwriters Association International). Visits Washington, D.C., to meet with members of the Senate and the House of Representatives to discuss issues facing songwriters.

2004   *Living The Rock 'n Roll Dream, THE ADVENTURES OF BUZZ CASON* , Buzz's biography is released, published by Hal Leonard. Buzz makes over fifty stops in fifteen states promoting the book.

2005   Nominated to Nashville Songwriters Hall Of Fame. Good friend Jerry Reed is inducted into the prestigious list of songwriters.

2006   Travels extensively in the U.S., The UK and Ireland in support of his book and recordings.

2007   Festival appearances include Larry Joe Taylor's Texas Music Festival, Tommy Alverson's Family gathering and Michael Hearne's Barndance Weekend in Taos NM.

2008   Appointed as a member of the Board Of Trustees, Campbellsville University, Campbellsville, Kentucky.

2009   Travels to Soldotna, Alaska for a hospital benefit cocert with songwriter and Alaska resident, Bonnie Nichols.

2010   Produces neo-rockabilly artist, Jesse Couch from Covington , Georgia. Completes first novel.

2011   Plays golf and sings in Randy Owen's Celebrity Golf Tournament and Concert in Alabama. Co-headlines Keith Sykes Songwriter Weekend with Roger Cook in Hot Springs AR. Begins recording of his fourth Americana/ Roots/Rock album in Anthony Crawford's Daphne AL studio and at home in Creative Workshop.

ACKNOWLEDGMENTS

To my parents, Rosa and Roy Cason, your love and inspiration are always with me. I am so thankful that my life has been so greatly blessed by family. Peggy, our children Tammy, Kristy (and Tim), Leah (and Chad), Taylor, Parker, and our grandchildren, Ashton Grace Wise, Rachel Neely Wise, Piper Cason Steen and Romy June Steen. You mean more to me than words can say. To my Victoria, thanks always for your love and support. I love you all dearly and I have come to know the true meaning of everlasting love because of you.

Over the years, numerous producers, songwriters, record company executives, singers, musicians, fellow publishers, engineers, deejays, promotional people, advisors, counselors, managers, agents and business associates and all of whom I treasure as friends have crossed my path and in so many diverse and helpful ways. The following are just a handful of the folks who have shared their talents and love with me and I am so blessed and grateful to know them. I regret there are absolutely too many to mention, but included in this very special group are:

Love and thanks to the original band of The Casuals: Richard Williams, Billy Smith, Johnny McCreery, Chester Power, and Clarence Wittinmeier. Additional members of the band I performed with included Joe Watkins, Tony Moon, Bobby Watts, Wayne Moss, Bobby Myers, Perry Potts, and Ray "Snuffy" Smith. Also gratitude to the originators of the music, Chuck Berry, Bo Diddley, and the blues greats who influenced all of us in such a powerful way: Joe Turner, Bobby "Blue" Bland, Little Walter, B.B. King, and Jimmy Reed.

Everyone who has been brave enough to attempt a co-write with me, all the musicians and singers who I have played live with or made recordings with, those who have simply encouraged and supported me and the fans who have come to shows, or bought the records.

To mention a few others who have encouraged me over the years and mean so much to me: Buzz Arledge, Eddy Arnold, Anthony Crawford, Dan Penn, Spooner Oldham, Donnie Fritts, Billy Swan, Rick Hall, Keith Sykes, Chips Moman, Charlie Black, Bobby Fischer, Mac Gayden, Bob Robison, Snuff Garrett, Kelso Herston, Bill Beasley, Bill Justis, Ron and Linda Chancey, Larry Butler, Tim Hinkley, Bucky Lindsey, Wayne Jackson, H. Jackson Brown, Randy Goodrum, Steve Gibson, Brent Maher, Todd Cerney, Travis Turk, Joe Funderburk, Richard E. Carpenter and all past Dartz band members, Johnny MacRae, Brenda Lee and Ronnie Shacklett, Austin Roberts, Bob Montgomery Robert K. Oermann, John T. and Mardi Parker, Carol Lindsey Vincent, Greg Hill, Jerry Carrigan, Paul Hampton, Jim Riordon, Jerry Kennedy, Richard Tinsley, Chance Martin, Herbert Graham, Pepper Martin, Gary and Peggy Walker, Bill Lowery, Dr. John Gibson, Len Rossi, Joe Rossi, Dickey Lee, Freddy Weller, Jerry Reed, Chip Young, Danny Judd, Charlie Lamb, Tommy Allsup, Leon Russell, Ray Stevens, Ron Hicklin, Fred Foster, Sonny James, Cindy Walker, Billy Sherill, Bob McDill, Wayne Carson, Johnny Christopher, Scotty Moore, Wade Conklin, Steve Gibb, Joey Smith, Kenny Rogers, Tom Douglas, Jesse Couch, Richard Leigh, Guy Gilchrist, Charlie Lamb, Aaron Sherz, Clifford Curry, Robert Knight, Steve Jarrell, Randy Layne and the Sons of the Beach and all the other classic rock artists who are always willing to help others, Francis Preston, Connie Bradley, Carl P. Mayfield, Jack Clement, Alamo Jones, Jeremy Tepper, Steve Popovich Sr. and Jr., and to mention a few of my Texas buddies: Larry Joe Taylor, Tommy Alverson, Davin James, Matt Martindale, Dallas Wayne, Brian Hofeldt and the Derailers, Susan Gibson, Kelly McGuire, Don Burke and Mark Gibson. Delbert McClinton, Paul Tull, Debbie Hupp, James Campbell, Rex Schnelle, Michael Hearne, Thom Schuyler, Chris and Lynne Cargen, Kim Patton-Johnson, Robert Deaton, George Flanigan, Chip Emerson, Joe and Bonnie Taggart, Mark Wright, Ron Solleveld, Bergen White, Bob Beckham, Billy Tagg and The Coaches, Art Fine, Rip Lay, Jerry Wexler, Tupper Saussy, Josh Sutherland, Bucky Wilkin, Everyone at NSAI, Betty Clark, Jerry Winfield and the Thursday Morning Gang , the family of GIFT and to believers everywhere, Michael Carter and everyone at Campbellsville University, my cousins Robert and Kenneth and Mark Jordan and all my Kentucky kinfolks. Ann and Rodney Young, Bob and Christine Denney, Lisa and Jeff Lassiter, my Aunt Betty, Uncle Bobby Dunaway, and all my other kinfolks.To Richard Crichton, thanks for your friendship and the wonderful photographs. To Chris Tibbott for your friendship and fabulous art and to your son, Terry Tibbott and all my racing team buddies over the years, for the cool memories. Speed lives!

To my legal advisors including Bob Epstein, Rush Hicks, David Risner, Ben McLane, Reid Street and Tom Taylor. Bankers and financial folks, Lori Stone, Louis Glaser, Cleston Daniels, Aurora Daniels, Chuck Akersloot and Royce Cannon. In Santa Rosa Beach, James Duren, and Michelle Eason. Also Bill Davis and the partners, , many thanks for putting up with me!

Finally, I'd also like to recognize as great pioneers of music in Nashville, the late Owen Bradley and Chet Atkins. These greatly talented men opened many doors for all of us.

PERMISSIONS AND PHOTO CREDITS

LYRIC PERMISSIONS

ARDEE AVENUE
Lyrics used by permission
Buzz Cason Publications, LLC—ASCAP
Sony, ATV Music Publishing—BMI

MY LOVE SONG FOR YOU
Lyrics used by permission
Buzz Cason Publications, LLC—ASCAP

IN THE BEGINNING
(A SIGN OF THE TIMES)
Lyrics used by permission
Buzz Cason Publications, LLC—ASCAP
Let There Be Music – BMI

ONE NIGHT IN MEMPHIS
Lyrics used by permission
Buzz Cason Publications, LLC—ASCAP

AN AMERICAN SATURDAY NIGHT
Lyrics used by permission
Buzz Cason Publications, LLC—ASCAP
Careers, BMG Music Publishing

TIGER AGO-GO
Lyrics used by permission
Buck Wilkin Publishing

LITTLE GREEN APPLES
Lyrics used by permission
Universal Polygram Music Publishing

1963

Lyrics used by permission
Thomas Leslie and Cliff Crofford
EMI UNART

(THEY ALL CALL HER) LA BAMBA
Lyrics used by permission
Zygote Publishing

EVERLASTING LOVE
Lyrics used by permission
EMI Music Publishing

LOVE'S THE ONLY HOUSE
Lyrics used by permission
Buzz Cason Publications, LLC—ASCAP
MCA/Sony Music Publishing—BMI

TIN CUP CHALICE
Lyrics used by permission
Let There Be Music

HONEY
Lyrics used by permission
Universal Polygram

PHOTO CREDITS

- Photos courtesy of The Buzz Cason Collection on pages: v, 1, 4, 12, 20, 24, 26, 27, 39, 40, 41, 45, 53, 54, 54, 59, 66, 77, 88, 91, 91, 98, 98, 99, 107, 108, 111, 112, 112, 113, 114, 114, 116, 120, 120, 125, 143, 149.

- Photos courtesy of Aaron Brown Collection on pages: 7, 119.

- Photo courtesy of Beth Gwynne on page: 121.

- Photos courtesy of Richard Crichton on pages: 106, 107, 111, 119,124

- Photo courtesy of ASCAP on page: 117.

- Photo courtesy of Tommy Marchman on page: 11.

- Photos courtesy of Liberty Records on pages: 115, 126, 129.

- Photo courtesy of Superior Photo Services, Birmingham, AL. on page: 52.

- Photo courtesy of Steve Bonner on page: 125.

- Photo courtesy of Rufus Dodson on page: 73.

- Photo courtesy of BMI Archives, 1996 on page: 141.

- Photo courtesy of Donna Fritts on page: 96.

- Photo courtesy of Ray Allen Photography on page: 100.

- Photo courtesy of Wanda Pojar on page: 105.

- Photo courtesy of Grammys on page: 105.

INDEX

Premiere
http://www.premiere.fastpencil.com